Testimonials

"Improv is much more than a fun team-building activity for my company. The ability of my team to learn how to be present in discussions and trust the truth and power of their ideas has become a distinct competitive advantage for my business. Adam is a master at making the experience fun and connecting the 'play' with the real-world value it delivers. If you have the good fortune of working with Adam & his organization, DO IT NOW! Your staff, clients and bottom line will thank you for it."

> - Brian Handrigan,
> Co-Founder and CEO,
> Avocado St. Louis, MO USA

"Adam is absolutely spot on with incorporating improv skills in your business. We use it a lot. It helps us to focus, stay, in the moment, and to open up the ideas. The creativity flows easier and your team enjoys the process"

> - Gary Vaynerchuk,
> CEO, Vayner Media, Global

"If you need your team to think on their feet, anticipate and creatively respond to the tough questions your customers and co-workers throw at them, Adam Sietz is the answer. My staff found that preparation and improvisational thinking were the keys to doing business better. I recommend Adam without hesitation."

> - Susan Lindner
> Founder & CEO,
> Innovation Storytellers, NYC, USA

"My experience with Adam has been wonderful. We have worked together on many of our Global events over the years. He is not only a fantastic facilitator, but also a top-notch keynote speaker and world-class host/emcee. I have seen what he has done with our group by bringing in humor and creative life skills to help us all grow. He brings a unique element that will help any executive team or company. Without any hesitation I fully recommend utilizing any or all of his services."

- Dean Lindal, VP,
EO, YPO & GSEA, Global

"Comedy in the business world is an elusive commodity. If anyone can incorporate comedy in consulting, Adam is your man. He has a gift with humor as a tool in communicating and in living."

- Frank Sweeney
Owner Sweeney Group Inc.

"Adam has become a huge asset to my company. He was so worthy, I nominated him for the Friars Club Board of Directors. He has helped raise the ability of the club and my team to learn how to be focused and present in meetings, and trust in the truth and power of their ideas. This has become a distinct competitive advantage for my business. Adam is a master at making the experience fun and connecting the 'play' with the real-world value it delivers. If you have the good fortune of attending one of his keynotes, or any way of working with Adam & his organization, don't be a yutz. DO IT NOW! Your staff, clients, and bottom line will thank you for it."

- Norman King
Founder & CEO,
American Marketing Complex, NYC

"Mostly"
The ^ True Confessions of a Successful
Former *Really Fat Guy with ADHD
(*Currently in Fat Guy Remission)
Who Vanquished Self Doubt and is Now Living His Dreams

Forward by **Peter Shankman** NY Times Best Seller & Global Influencer

UNSCRIPTED
$UCCESS WITH
IMPROVISATIONAL THINKING

Secrets of How to Sell It...

...Whatever your "IT" is?
Get Them to Buy into "IT" With a Smile!
IT = Your Idea – Your Product – Your Service – Your Opinion

ADAM LEE SIETZ

Sietz's Bureau, EaglesTalent.com at 1-973-313-9800, or visit any of his WebSietz. Please come to say Hi at: adamsietz.com, comedyation.com, improvolutions.com or bighugproductions.com

Cover Art by Nabin Karna

Manufactured in the USA 10 9 8 7 6 5 4 3 2 1

The Library of Congress has cataloged the hardcover Edition as follows

Adam Sietz - Unscripted $uccess with Improvisational Thinking Secrets of How to Sell it. Whatever your IT is.

ISBN 979-8-9900330-0-9 (pbk)
ISBN 979-8-9900330-1-6 (eBook)
ISBN 979-8-9900330-2-3 (hardcover)

Photo By Scott Singer

I hope you get a kick out of my book

Dedication

For my entire family!

But especially my wife Melissa...I call her Mylissa

and

My three delicious children Sophie, Noah, and BenJamin

Te' & La, Mom & Dad

I love you all as high as the sky,

As deep as the ocean,

and forever and ever!

To Najia, my lead whip-cracker and Adventure Guide

&

To those of you out there still doubting yourself.

Stop it!

Duh?!

Acknowledgments

For me to get where I always wanted, it took a lot of hard work, a few helpful pushes, and a kick…or three in the A$$ along the way. I want to acknowledge all of my Family, Friends, Clients, and colleagues. I thank all of the people who kept me moving towards my path.

Too many names to mention. You all know exactly who you are, and know that I love you all…Well, maybe not you Todd…but everyone else. Oh, and a special mention to Judy. She is gone but her Judyisms and wise words live on @ judywinchell.com Oh and a huge thank you to the creators of Pizza, Dumplings and Burgers.

I thank those of you who have affected me, rejected me, loved me, pushed me, famushed me, bashed me, smashed me, fed me, said me, folded me, scolded me, thought me, taught me, bought me, fought me, and for me. With you all in my world, I am richer! Without you all, I would be much less than I am. I also want to thank YOU. Yup you, the good-looking person reading this sentence right now. And, may I say, you do have beautiful eyes…Prrr.

Thank YOU for your willingness to decide to open this book. For putting your trust, time, and energy into reading (hopefully all of) the words of an odd, compassionate, empathetic, neurodiverse, former really fat guy (currently in fat guy remission).

These pages are filled with my experiences (Good and Bad), my thoughts, stories, opinions, advice, blabbing on, yada…yada… yada…and some supportive tools, exercises, and knowledge to help you be that better you I wish, *and know* YOU CAN and YOU WILL be!

Acknowledge the people in your life today and yesterday. Do it now! Some of them won't always be here to receive your love. Tell those you love how much and why you love them. You may find out what it is about YOU they love

Thank YOU all!

Letter From Author

Dear Reader,

Allow me to introduce myself. My name is…Adam. Some call me Ad, Adz, Adam "One" Size "Fits All", Dude, Dad, Mom? Or my favorite, HEY YOU! I am a man who has spent a lifetime Embracing the Extraordinary Power of Humor, the Coolness of Creativity, and the Gift of Neurodiversity. In the following pages, you will embark on your life-changing journey, exploring the wondrous world inside of that mushy computer safely encased in your skull. You will learn ways to increase your mental agility through the tenets of Improvisational Thinking and how it can transform not just your approach to sales, and business, but your entire outlook in life.

My story is unique, woven from the threads of comedy and creativity, deficits, disappointments, and disorder. I was born into an entertainment family, my father was a comedian turned television producer, and my mother was a professional with connections to legends like Sammy Davis Jr, Sid Caesar, Ed Sullivan, and Jackie Gleason. She even turned away Elvis's advances on the same night she met my dad.

At an early age, my parents were told my IQ was off the charts, Mensa level, and then proceeded to label me with "Severe ADHD". For years, I grappled with and believed I was a deficit and a disorder. But, as life unfolded, I realized that I possessed something truly special—a hyper-awareness that allowed me to see the world in a way others couldn't.

My journey took me from a school for children with learning disabilities to the corporate world. Then into production, the entertainment business, and eventually, to the biggest of all stages! Over the years, I've worn many hats — salesman, comedian, actor, producer, writer, voice artist, speaker, facilitator, emcee, contest judge, burger maven, lover of ice cream, substitute little league coach and so much more. I've lent my voice to beloved animated characters, and campaigns, and made people laugh around the globe.

This book is not about my story; it's about yours. It's about the potential you already have deep within you. I will help you trust your intuition, stop censoring or squelching your instant thoughts, take more risks, and seriously raise your ability to respond to the unexpected.

Using the skills I gained from well over 1,000 stage time hours performing, I will help you tap into the knowledge you've already gathered throughout a lifetime of experiences. I will promise you this, if you follow these processes or at least some of the ideas laid out here, YOU will completely change those things that need to change. You will transform your life and business into your vision filled with abundance. You see, humor mixed with the ability and agility to improvise, helps you perform better. Improv is not just about comedy; it's a powerful tool for communication, problem-solving, and innovation.

In these pages, I will share with you the secrets of how improvisation can be applied to sales and business. Through anecdotes, examples, exercises, and practical tips, I aim to bring you not only education but also joy. The ability to improvise can make your interactions with clients, colleagues, friends, and loved ones, be more engaging and enjoyable.

I have experienced the highs and lows of life, both in business and personal matters. I've faced financial challenges, navigated career changes, and relationship trauma, and I've emerged stronger and wiser. Through it all, I've come to understand that staying present, flexible, funny, and kind is more than just a skill; it's a way of life.

From deep depression, weighing over 420 lbs., and constantly being told I was less than (mostly by myself), to living my dreams. I sincerely want to help you to do the same. I want to guide you toward finding the fun and joy in every relationship you have, whether it's with coworkers, superiors, family, friends, or strangers. The principles offered on these pages can and will enhance all these connections, making your life richer, happier more often, and way more fulfilling.

As you read through these pages, remember that I'm not here to brag about my accomplishments, but to share my conviction that you too can embrace the transformative power of Improvisational Thinking. My mission is to assist you in breaking down barriers, vanquishing self-doubt, shedding excuses, finding order, self-accountability, and boldly pursuing your goals, whatever they may be.

In closing, I invite you to join me on this journey, to explore the limitless potential that's already within you. As you delve into the world of improvisation, may you find valuable insights and the inspiration to make a positive change in your life and business and hopefully smile here and there…maybe a chuckle, guffaw, or a laugh.

With love, humor, creativity, and a whole lot of heart.

Big Hugs
Adam Lee Sietz

PS: While 86% of these words were being etched in font, I was NOT wearing pants.

How To Read This Book

Well, I must say, I'm blown away to know you are holding this book. I can tell you I am serious and I am told, I am funny, so I do believe this book will be funious. But, forget about me, because it's YOU reading the words on the pages to come, so the real superstar here is… drumroll, please...YOU! That's right! Do you wanna win? Yes! Then…WIN! Just remember to Practice!

In this book, I'm going to get you P.A.C.K.E.D. and ready to go. I will help you by being your very own, been there done that, laugh-inducing, transformation-commanding, farting sherpa. Now, I get it, taking a few minutes to ask someone to do some of the exercises shown might make you feel silly, awkward, and uncomfortable. That's Okay. Do it anyway. When you practice with another person, you double the learning and triple the fun (I'm adding myself as a participant in that fun…I wrote this stuff). You may not want to do them, but I do promise you from the bottom of my fart, if you do, with time and consistency YOU can make YOU feel like YOU can do the things YOU haven't done…yet! So, here's my brilliant plan: Read a chapter a day…a week…an Olympic year? If it's the latter, your lack of action and effort won't affect me. If you do something today, another thing tomorrow, and why not sprinkle in one in the day after that, and so on, and so on. It'll be easy peasy (I know that was cheesy), right? OK Maybe simple, but not always easy.

These practices are not just window dressing. They're the secret sauce to unleashing the power in YOU, unleashing your inner funny, and increasing confidence in your game. Whether it be sales, teaching, training, or just listening, you will be turbocharging every nook and cranny of your home and business life. I mean, you won't have customers, you will have friends…that need what you can do and will pay you for what You do.

So, here's the deal – don't speed-read through this book like you're on a caffeine rush or feel the need to rush to the lavatory to drop a deuce. Please take these exercises, and games and give'em a whirl. If you do practice what I'm dishing out you'll get a return on investment that's more valuable than finding a golden ticket in a chocolate bar. 18 times more valuable, to be precise.

Oh, and remember, lightning doesn't strike once, and neither should you with this book. My advanced students have said 'They've heard and read the stuff in this book more than once, and every time they read this stuff or hear it repeated, they always catch on to something, or remember new tidbits of applicable knowledge. They practically have more "aha" moments in their sleep. Each time you revisit the material, the repetition helps you to learn your way. For example, in an epic video game, after the first turtle shell or rolling barrel hits you, killing that turn, you learn from that tragedy by knowing when to jump the next time. Certain things, actions, thoughts must be done over and over again to attain mastery and unlock another level.

Instead of power-ups, you get remarkable transformative results. Proven techniques and thought processing that will help you develop the mindset you want to solidify. You will see stuff getting done. You will have more order, organization, and self-accountability. Won't it be great to know exactly where you keep your stuff? You will always make it to wherever you are meeting someone, on time or better yet early, and you will never drive away and realize you left your wife in the Dome Hepot store (no free plugs here). That would be sweet,right?

So, as you flip through these pages, remember this: I'm not just hoping you'll get a chuckle or two. I'm banking on you receiving some valuable life benefits, buckets of happiness, laughter, and creating many new smiles. Oh yeah, that was top-level cheesy. I know. Here's some more…

Give yourself an extreme makeover and improve your business and civilian life substantially by diving headfirst into the stuff I've laid out in the following font.

WARNING: It'll be like learning an instrument, if you want to sound good, you must practice!

Practice! Practice! Practice like you're about to win the air bass championship, like you're about to ask that special someone to marry you, or like asking and hoping for forgiveness for what you did at last year's end-of-year holiday Christmas party.

Experience and share the magic of these exercises. Do your best to work on some of these games/exercises with a partner. Once you begin, please stay present and DON'T THINK TOO MUCH! LISTEN, TRUST WHAT COMES. GO and DO IT! Trust in what instantly pops into your thoughts and DO NOT immediately censor it. You may learn how to laugh at yourself and in time, your abs won't hurt as much – not just from laughing, but from all those sit-ups you won't have to do all the time.

Enjoy every moment of this wild ride YOU are currently living. I truly hope this book helps you improve your skill set and sets roots with repetition.

Therefore…Please Remember to:

- Practice (I know…but it is important)
- Say Yes.
- Go! Do IT!
- Experience NOW.
- Laugh.

- Enjoy.
- Thank your tribe.

Most importantly, I thank you for taking this adventure with me. Thank you for choosing laughter, growth, and hopefully, action. And, Expect Unscripted Success for YOU!

Information Offered in This Book

Relax and imagine, for a moment…NO, not me in a tube top! Please take a moment to imagine a world where business and sales weren't just about number$, $preadsheets, and cold, sterile transaction$. No. Instead, picture a world where coffee still costs less than $1.00, every interaction is infused with warmth, spontaneity,humor, and a genuine connection. That, my friend, is the world I want to introduce you to—a world where Improvisational Thinking reigns supreme and self-worth is actualized! But sorry, I am wrong. Coffee will still cost you $3.00 plus a guilt tip.

The Ultimate Purpose

After briefly contemplating retirement at 50, I came to the obvious conclusion that I couldn't sit around and do nothing, eating way too much, hacking up the local golf courses, and not wearing pants. Oh yeah, I was also lacking the level of funding to allow me to support my family to relax for the next 30-40 years. As you read on you will see that a $ is not what drives me. Hopefully, it doesn't drive you either. Happiness, Love, The Little Wins, and laughter do drive me.

I have been very blessed. I've learned, I've earned, and now I wish to return. At the core of my life mission from here on out lies a belief that my ultimate purpose is to put smiles on faces and help others to do the same. To find where, who, and how I can be of service in helping them conquer fear and self-doubt.

Remember what I said earlier, I am a Hyper Aware Individual. My brain is faster than the average brain, I am…ok you can call it

ADHD. You will see, I can go off-topic a little bit here and there…Ok, a lot…If it bothers you…Well, Excuuuse Meee! If it really bothers you, think of it as a collection of individual thoughts assembled in a way that could be understood…I think? I am just …Look a Firetruck!

If you are a grammar critic, feel free to correct any errors you catch on your copy :o) I spent less than one semester in college. For me, the words are not the Punctuation, Syntax, Diazeugmas, or Paraprosdokians (look them up, I just did); Those never stuck…so…just let it go.

I love books that allow me to finish a section or a chapter when I have a few free minutes. Remember Dan Browns, DaVinci code? 101 Chapters. It felt like each chapter was a scene in the film running in my mind. Perfect for a post-egg and coffee visit to the potty. That's right, you can read a bit while you take a shit. So, think of it like this: take each piece on its own as many are stand-alone thoughts ranging from Sales to Self-Improvement, Neurodiversity, Saying Yes, Organization, Weight loss, Farting, yada yada yada…Please just take it for what it is. Thoughts put on paper by some guy who would like to help you with your "Inner Me" stuff. Some will resonate, some may not. I am not a linear thinker. I use a lot of …'s for the reader to take a longer beat than a coma…see?

These actions I've written within the pages have improved me, made me kinder to others, and made some amazing Deals, Sales, and Wins. You will see it if you get up every morning…make your bed…then get PACKED with LARRY to go out into the world and kick its ass. I remind myself that every endeavor should be driven by the desire to help and serve others. Helping others helps me. It is precisely this philosophy that led to my Unscripted $uccess. Here we go…

Table of Contents

Foreword

It is with immense excitement that I pen this foreword for "Unscripted $uccess," a book that is not just a manuscript but a journey through the vibrant life of Adam Lee Sietz. I have had the pleasure of knowing Adam for several years, and if there's one thing that stands out about him, it's his infectious humor and remarkable talent in his multiple endeavors. This book is a reflection of the man behind those endeavors – witty, insightful, and incredibly resilient.

"Unscripted $uccess" is more than just a book; it's a guide, a companion, and a mirror to our own lives. Adam, with his unique blend of humor and wisdom, takes us through the highs and lows of his life, teaching us the power of improvisational thinking. This is not just Adam's story; it's a narrative that resonates with anyone who has ever faced challenges, self-doubt, or the desire to pursue their dreams against all odds.

One of the most compelling aspects of this book is Adam's ability to transform personal anecdotes into universal life lessons. As a reader, you will find yourself laughing, nodding in agreement, and occasionally pausing to reflect on your own life. The book is an invitation to embrace the unexpected, to find humor in the mundane, and to approach life with a renewed sense of curiosity and adventure.

Adam's journey is a testament to the power of persistence, creativity, and, most importantly, believing in oneself. His story is a reminder that success is not always scripted and that sometimes, the most profound lessons come from unscripted moments. "Unscripted $uccess" encourages us to break free from the shackles of conventional thinking and to explore the limitless possibilities and potential within each of us.

As you turn the pages of this book, I invite you to join Adam on this incredible journey. Whether you are looking for inspiration, a good laugh, or practical wisdom, "Unscripted $uccess" has something for everyone. It is my honor to introduce you to Adam's world – a world where humor, heart, and hard-won wisdom come together to create something truly extraordinary.

Peter Shankman
peter@shankman.com
New York City

Six-time bestselling author
Two-time NY Times bestseller
Serial entrepreneur
Founder of HERO (& HARO)
Mental Capital Consulting

Act 1:
Unleashing the
Positive Power Play

Yes!
Don't Overthink it! Now?

Chapter 1
Introduction

* * *

A Life Committed to Service

My journey has been one of discovery and growth, successes and failures, grief and happiness. As my journey continues, IT is fueled by the belief that Improvisational Thinking (IT) can be a powerful force for positive change. I've dedicated my life to preaching the gospel of IT and to helping as many people as I can to break free from the shackles of self-doubt, living as an introvert, or being afraid to ask for something you want. Can't pick up a telephone and make a sales call? Are you or do you know anyone who is painfully shy, needlessly fearful of speaking in public or to the opposite sex? That was me.

I grew leaps and bounds by facing the unknown. Before I took control back, I also grew my waistline. I was a size TENT. By empowering myself, and now others, with the skills needed to develop strong relationships, better communication, and presence to ace press interviews, navigate meetings with new clients, and gain a higher % of closed deals. I want to help you master the delicate art of living that life you desire, business negotiations, make more sales, and find humor everywhere. IT can also increase your chances of not only getting that sale but maybe a first date, second date…and then…it's you and Missy sittin' in a tree…K…I…S…you get the point.

The Mission Unveiled

So, what exactly is my mission? In simple terms, it's to create a friendly social atmosphere where individuals can shed their inhibitions, shyness, and discomfort, all while honing their skills crucial for success in the world. It's all about transforming every interaction into an opportunity for growth and connection. A great byproduct of this mission is when all of your needs $tart to come your way.

Here's the exciting part: IT is the key to achieving this mission. It's the secret sauce that can turn even the most mundane business encounter into a delightfully funny, bonding, informal, and fruitful exchange. Ending with a Big Hug. Thats my goal every time.

Look at me, I've Got ADHD

Selling isn't about being perfect; it's about being authentically you. We'll delve into the importance of authenticity in sales. You don't need to fit into a cookie-cutter mold to succeed. No script is needed. They are too restrictive.

Embracing your unique qualities, even something like Autism, ADHD, blindness or hearing impairment has particularly enhanced senses and skills that can be an asset in many ways when channeled correctly. Let's discover how your quirks can be your strengths.

Midway through the second grade I was getting in trouble…a lot. Flipping desks and distracting the class. After a couple of fights, many hours sitting in the principal's office, and getting caught showing Lisa Dwyer my privates, they said "...he needs to be evaluated.' So, I was evaluated by what they called the Child Study Team. In the end, my parents were told "Adam has an IQ of a genius! Mensa level...but...he has severe ADHD. Then delivered lines to my parents, with me sitting right there. This little so-called genius could hear every word as they were etched into my belief records and stored deep within my Brains Operating Super System (BOSS). I think labeling any child with terms that include, DEFICIT and DISORDER is simply wrong. This label stuck, and it affected me throughout most of my life.

30 years ago...I called bullshit! I decided to personally re-diagnose myself with: "HYPER-AWARENESS" and decided to completely change the direction of my life path. Yup. I am an ADHD poster child. I am neurodiverse. I do not believe it is a bad thing. That's just me. To most others, the perception of ADD or ADHD is a bad thing. Some will even say "I am so sorry". It happened to me just 11 days ago (Yes, we can be extremely specific).

I was picking up an audiobook called "Delivered from Distraction" written by Edward M. Hallowell, M.D and John J. Ratey. I had just finished a fantastic book written by Peter Shankman, a fellow Hyper-Aware entrepreneur, and the man who wrote my foreward.

His book is called "Faster than Normal: Turbocharge your Focus, productivity, and Success with the Secrets of the ADHD Brain". Peter is a kind, funny, and brilliantly wise soul. This best-selling author truly says it all with the perfect title he gave that Book.

I knew I had Hyper-Awareness, or as he called it "A Faster than Normal Brain". Check out his FTN podcast too. We had fun.

Faster Than Normal Episode #: 85 - Adam Sietz

Award-Winning Comedian, Actor, and ADHD Poster Boy:

https://tinyurl.com/bdcsjeta:

We instantly hit it off. This was a helpful book for me. It not only
4

gave me strong tips, and new knowledge and generated some new ideas, this book validated my feelings on the entire topic. So many of the tips Peter's book gave me, I had naturally adopted on my own through my half century on this orbiting ball all of us reside. Maybe not all? Aliens?

Short story, our brain works faster than the typical brain. The brain is beyond comprehension. Who cares? Trust yours to work for you!

What does this have to do with Sales performance and creatively effective communication? I am preaching the gospel of focusing on the NOW! Those of us with this "affliction" (HA to that definition), we do best in the RIGHT NOW! Read on and you will see what I mean.

Here is the longer-ish story. At 7 years old (way back in 1973) I was a handful. My parents were asked to remove me from the local public school for bad behavior and being a constant distraction. I was diagnosed with ADHD and put into a special school for "Children with Learning Disabilities".

I was part of the main Rutgers/Johnson study done by Dr. Larry Silver researching this "Disability". I've been calling myself an ADHD Lab Rat and Poster Boy for years.

To me, the idea of labeling a child with a diagnosis that includes those words "Diagnosis", "Deficit" and "Disorder", sucked. I didn't know what those words meant or what just happened. All I knew, was starting Monday, I was going to be going to a different school. Or should I say a School for Different's?

Looking back today, being labeled with a disorder of deficit and describing it as a disability was bullshit! It is just wrong. It is not at all helpful. I believe it is damaging. I, and most kids that hear this medical term used to describe us, are able to find and read a dictionary. I looked up those 3 words. I also looked up "Sex", but that is another book altogether.

Diagnosis: di·ag·no·sis, diəg'nō·səs, *noun*

The identification of the nature of **an illness or other problem by** examination of the symptoms "Early diagnosis and treatment are essential"

Deficit: def·i·cit, 'defəsət, *Noun*

noun: **deficit**; *plural noun:* **deficits**

The amount by which something, especially a sum of money, is too small.

Synonyms: **shortfall, deficiency, shortage, negative**,amount, **loss, debt**, arrears

Antonyms: Surplus

In sports: The amount or score by which a team or individual is **losing**.

Technical Term: a **deficiency or failing, especially in a neurological or psychological function**

Disorder:

dis·or·der, dis'ôrdər ', noun: **disorder plural** *noun:* **disorders**

"Eating disorders. a disruption of the healthy or normal functioning; of normal physical or mental functions; a disease or abnormal condition.

synonyms: **infection, complaint, condition, affliction, malady, sickness, illness, ailment, infirmity, irregularity**, "a blood disorder"

So, I had a Disability? What's a disability? Being a devoted of the New York Mets? (Rimshot)

Not only did I look up the definitions, but I also looked up the synonyms and antonyms. It was rather unpleasant. Some of those words were even worse. This shitty label (Diagnosis of ADHD) told me I was less than. I believed this to be true for many years.

I always wanted to become a performer, so I became one! I have been so blessed too. I've been so fortunate to live my childhood dreams, and then some. I have accomplished many of the things I had on my bucket list from way back in my early childhood through my recent goals. I did most of it weighing over 420 lbs. Other than not being at my goal weight just yet, I am another person. More like I lost an entire other person. I am a whole lot thinner than I was. I am currently 170 lbs. less than I was less than a decade ago, I am a very happy former really fat guy (currently in fat guy remission). I am also human, so are you. Or are you? Aliens?

You are here and I want to share my experience of how Improvisation changed my life. Drastically!

The Power of YES: A Yes Can Change Your Life

Back before my father met my mother, and she said…YES! He and his best friend Barry were performers. Seymour Sietz, and Barry Schwartz, "The Stewart Brothers". They were a great team, funny, and fairly successful at the very young age of only 16.

Their act was a record act. It was inspired by Jerry Lewis. Jerry would come out with a record player. He would begin in silence simply turning on the record player and setting himself. Jerry

7

begins to deliver perfectly choreographed physicality, while he lip-syncs to it. By the way, it was the booming voice of a female opera singer. His facial and body movements had the audience in hysterics.

Dad and Barry did something similar, but theirs was to the music of Spike Jones. Spike had a wacky band of musicians playing odd instruments. Instruments like a toilet bowl tuba or a kitchen sink trombone. Way before Stomp, Spike made music out of anything. He would insert unique sounds like animal noises, gunshots, crashing plates and car horns. This was as far from opera, as you can imagine.

They toured with some of the greats of their day. Buddy Hackett, Alan King, Jackie Vernon (Frosty), and many more. They even made it to the Ed Sullivan Show.

Eventually, Barry got married. Unfortunately, his new bride wanted him to leave the act and get a real job. My dad tried to continue with someone else and then on his own, but without Barry, it just wasn't the same so he went and got a real job too.

Barry ended up the founder of one of the biggest public relations firms in the toy industry, and my dad became an Executive Producer. I hated that he traveled so much. Production days only came about after many many phone calls putting it all together. That was when I learned that a Producer is a glorified word for a master salesman. Life was good.

Fast forward 30 years. My mother is now an Executive Director for the Miss Universe organization. She ran Miss New York, Miss New Jersey, Miss New York Teen, and Miss New Jersey Teen for Miss USA, Mrs. America and Miss and Mrs. World. Dad helped develop and produce the national broadcast. Dad and Barry would reunite and resurrect the act a few times a year covering the entertainment for my mom's show. It was great for all of us because we got to see him perform. My sisters and I got to see a different side of him. When he was up there, you could feel him shine. You can see the joy flowing out of him. Truly some of our favorite moments.

Winter of 93', the weather was horrible. Barry was not able to make it to the resort for the show. My dad decided it was time for me to do the act with him. He asked, I said no. I will mess it up dad. No way. I'm too fat. I have never been upfront on stage before, and I didn't want to embarrass myself. This was the first time on a stage, let alone in front of 500+ people. I was firm in my decision of no way.

The pressure began. After a couple of asks, my dad gave up. My sisters and mother, however, along with virtually the entire crew, and anyone else that was able to speak to me and tell me to do it. No. He wants you to do it. No. Your mom needs you to do it so the scheduled Entertainment can still go on. No! No! No!

After two days of rejecting the idea, I began to wonder what it would be like. I may have said NO once or twice more, but in the end, I did say *YES…

*Quick author, note – The moment I typed the above YES and the letters appeared on my laptop's screen, I got choked up. It still feels like it was yesterday. I miss him. I've never written this story down. So, seeing it put in words brought me right back to that moment. The wave of gratitude, and pride in that monumental decision to perform with him for the first…and last time ever. 30 years have passed yet it still kicks my ass.

Back to the story…

So, it's showtime, and now I am physically shaking. In about two minutes, the fear is boiling over. I am sure you've seen or perhaps experienced the line for a scary ride like a giant roller coaster.

You wait for what seems like forever. The un-comfortability rises. Just before it's your turn, it hits you hard. That wave of fear, anxiety, wanting to fight or flight. You're going to bow out. "Hey guys, um, I'm not feeling great. Maybe I got food poisoning. Now, feeling like a coward, disappointed, and embarrassed you quit. This is exactly what was happening to me. Moments before we were to be introduced, I said, "Dad, can you just do it by yourself? You've done it before? I've seen you do it alone." He said "I'd prefer not to, but I won't make you do it if you don't want to do it. I get it. I love you. It's OK." Ugh! Now I have to do it. I mean, come on! He truly was gold. Here goes! Joe Derose, our brilliant MC, introduced Dad alone. He welcomed the audience, said a couple of silly things, and called me up to the stage. My heart was beating at a pace of 1000 beats a minute, and I was still shaking. So much so that everyone in the audience could see, so I closed my eyes and embellished being ridiculously scared by really shaking in a much more exaggerated manner…Laughter rings out. To myself, "Huh? Was that for me?"

- *Five seconds in:* I took a deep breath or three, opened my eyes, and looked out at this giant audience filled with over 500 faces staring directly at me.
- *Ten seconds in:* Finally, I am focused and I'm ready, the shaking has stopped. My heart is now only beating 250 bpm. Suddenly, I realize I have seconds before it's my turn.
- *Fifteen seconds in:* I lip-synch my first line. More Laughter.
- "Holy schnikes! That one was for me!"

As the act went on, I felt more comfortable. So comfortable that by the time Dad was about to close out the bit, I ripped the microphone stand away from him, and closed out the song. At that moment I turned to my right to see the look on my dad's face of pure pride and joy. His son was now a Stewart Brother. As I turned back toward the audience, I was shocked to see them all standing up applauding loudly. Lee Stewart was born.

10

When we got backstage, he gave me a big hug and told me how proud he was. He asked if I would do it again, and I said maybe. He said, I'll take maybe. He hugged me again and we both went out to watch the rest of the show.

If I had stuck to my guns and my NO, instead of my saying YES, my life would be quite different than it is today. I say this with confidence because less than 30 days later, he died.

Suddenly my father was gone. I never got to make that maybe into a YES. I never got to perform with him again.

With this new reality, I was not only grieving, but afraid of what was to come. I was now responsible for the company he created. I did do it for a while longer and did well, but the truth was very clear to me. That day, 15 seconds into "Cocktails for Two", the universe, or G-d, if you prefer, hit me with a wave of appreciation, happiness, and a brand-new addiction to audience adoration.

It did not take long for me to jump into the pool of comedy. I decided to put an ad in the local newspaper to start a sketch comedy troupe. When I opened the paper to find the phone number to call, I saw there was already an ad posted by someone else looking to do the same thing. "Starting a sketch comedy troupe. Auditions this weekend". Being a young naïve amateur, my initial thought was "Oh shit! There's competition".

It took a few, but I quickly realized looking at that ad as competition was the wrong way. I flipped my thoughts. I decided to look at it in this positive way instead. Someone else has made it easier for me to achieve my goal. I have no clue at all what I am going to have to do, doing it alone may not be wise. Let's see...I picked up the phone and called the number in the ad. After a brief conversation and a few laughs, I asked him if he wanted to partner up and build it together. He said...what do you think? YES!

Now I will remind you that my Comedy experience was only limited to the one performance I did with my father. Okay well, I fudged it up a little by omission, but hey I had three options: 1.) Call him and tell him "I've never been on a stage other than the one time with my dad for approximately, 8 minutes and 12 seconds? Oh, and by the way, I was a sidekick lip-syncing to someone else's material"? No. Not that one. 2) Ask for an audition. Not me. Or...3) Sell IT! Bingo!

I listened to his vision; it was virtually the same as mine. After I charmed him into smiling. I then extracted a laugh to lock it in. I would share my Product...echeem...sales ability, and promotional and marketing skills and he would lead in direction. We would work together on casting, but he would have the final say regarding show format and accounting. I said YES. He said YES! Aaaand we're off to the races. Now, I am already in on whatever he was up to without ever auditioning. He was now in on whatever I was able to muster up for us.

Feeling the need to pull away from the career my dad had planned for me, I began working on fulfilling the plan he had originally wanted for himself, but had to cut it short and let it go. I was now, all in. I began transitioning into the man I am today.

Looking back on that day, I like to think G-d, (or the universe if You prefer) knew what had to happen for me to truly understand what my purpose in life was. Knowing my dad only had a month left on this earth and my needing to get up on that stage…on that day…at that moment, to have that life-altering experience that would plant the initial seed. A great example of the old saying: "Man plans, G-d Laughs". In this case of the funny, G-d laughs…literally.

Then there was another time I am now sure a seed was planted. A seed that would have at least dropped me in the middle of my Purpose, but…I SAID NO! Something that was meant to be, was blocked for over a decade. Blocked by my unwillingness to explore the opportunities or offers laid on my path.

FLASHBACK to 1982, I was a sophomore at Jersey's own East Brunswick High School. Hollyrock High. (Go Bears!) I was constantly in the main office for one thing or another. For the time my friend and I hid a dead trout in Mrs. Whatsherface's art cabinet. It was his idea. I supplied the dead fish and he stuck it under an art box full of colorful cray paper, googly eyes, and puffy balls nobody ever touched this box. Our thinking was it would take weeks and a build-up of some serious stink for her to find it. When we were accused, we denied it and said it had to be someone else.

The fact that my backpack smelled like the Fulton Street Fish Market did not help our case. Just for the record, Mrs. Whatsherface was a bigot, typically angry at the world, and for a few generations, she has been annually unadored by students.

One day, my guidance counselor had an idea. He had me talk to the East Brunswick High School Drama Teacher. His name was Elliot Taubenslag. He was well known in the area as he had been running the high school musicals in town for decades.

We spoke for a bit. He was very kind, funny, and supportive of my neurodiversity. He couldn't believe we had never met or that I had never participated in any of the on-stage, theatrical stuff. When he asked why? I said…I duhNO. Whenever my friends would tell me "Dude, you've got to do something in the talent show!" I said NO.

"Aye, let's do a Monty Python sketch on the senior variety show." NO. Whenever I was told, "You are a great drummer you should be in a band". NO. I did find some other players to jam in my basement, in My house, in My safe place. "Hey Adz, would you and your friends play at my party this weekend"? NO.

I had ZERO belief in myself. Zero confidence to attempt anything that would make me stand out. Looking back on it today, receiving the wonderful news the child study team laid on me in second grade, remember that sweet diagnosis of my disorder, being a deficit and seriously disabled? For decades I discontinued my skills, my inherited abilities, and my great ass, and my beautiful eyes. I was less than, so why even try? I always let my inner critic, self-doubt and paralyzing fear rip me off of all the memorable high school events. Football games? Nope. My Prom? Nope. Get to play the "I'll show you mine if you show me yours" game in the back corner of the ceramics room? …YES!

I lived life saying NO to way too many great experiences. Do you?

Perhaps it was the power of purpose, the universe, the lord above speaking to me through Mr. T? Amen! I said NO! I spent too much time in my head denying myself the joy I now know Mr. T wanted for me 40 years ago. I stopped wondering what could have been if I had been willing to step out and show my face, but I had said NO.

As we finished, Mr. Taubenslag grabbed this teeny tiny yellow pad and wrote down three words "Chicago City Limits", and a phone number. He peeled it off, stuck it on my notebook, and said "You are funny. I want you to call this number, tell them I sent you, and say you must take classes". When I got home, I immediately peeled what I found out was a new invention called a Post-it Note off my notebook. I had never seen one. It was pretty cool. Did I call the number? NO! I stuck it on the bottom of my mirror where it would reside for over a decade. Fast forward to 1995'ish. I quickly educated myself in the world of improv comedy by fire. We were ready but didn't have anywhere to perform. With a budget of $0.00, we found a great space. Pat found the head honcho of the Art Serve Auditorium in Ft. Lauderdale. They closed their doors at 6 pm on the weekend. So, he worked out a deal to use the space for pennies when it was not in use. They said YES!

About one year later, we had made a name for ourselves. Lots of great reviews and free press allowed us the opportunity to move into our own space. ComedySportz was open for business! Our little comedy troupe now ran our 250-seat club! I had a team and mentor who helped us learn and play with a bunch of world-class improvisers. I eventually left Florida in 1998 to be a professional performer in the Big Apple, NYC.

YES, is the most fruitful word in my vocabulary. When I asked my wife to marry me, she said YES. Each time we asked the doctor if our babies were healthy, he said YES. When I asked to be sent out as a professional actor, the manager, said YES. That yes, was given to me, knowing that I had absolutely zero training, other than performing some improv and stand-up comedy.

A quarter century later, I've lived my dream. You are reading this story, and now, I am sitting up in bed typing this part next to my sleeping wife and a gassy cat. I am hoping you are finding enough value. Wait, Wait! STOP! That's my inner critic questioning will it be good enough? Instead, I imagine asking YOU if you like what you've read so far. And guess what? This is my imaginary exchange, so I will have you wrap it up and say…YES!

Exercise – Please take a moment to think about some of the things, actions, inactions, experiences, offers, and opportunities in your life you said NO to. Maybe one or more that you eventually gave in and said yes to, finding out it was not as bad as you thought. Maybe you even liked it. Make a list of them. Are there any on that list you can rectify? If not, no worries. You have just unlocked a few examples of what to do next time that opportunity for a YES comes your way.

Reflecting on my past, I've recognized that my inclination to use "I can't" as an excuse was a choice, and understanding the power within "I won't" or "I can't" empowers us to navigate challenges and consciously influence the changes we want in our lives.

I Can't or I Won't = I Choose Not To

I always used "I Can't" as an excuse to NOT challenge myself. Have you? I will take it, you answered "Yes". We CAN choose to say I CAN'T or I WON'T. These statements are choices. Often, I can't or won't is the better choice and quite appropriate in many cases. For example, I could cross the double yellow line on the highway, but I won't. I can choose to strip down to nothing more than my underpants, or better yet, a bright orange Speedo, but I won't! Why don't I? Because I CHOOSE NOT TO! Not because I can't, but because it would not be the brightest thing to do. Saying I can't lose weight, or I can't pick up the phone and make that call, you are wrong. I won't stop that baby from crawling into rushing traffic. Saying I can't save the world may be a bit extreme…or is it!? Say "I can!" say "I will!

When you are facing challenges or changes, big or small, dig deep and ask yourself, why do I need to make the change? We are all changing every second of every minute of every day. We just don't notice the minutia. We also have the power to create change. We do it without knowing it.

Exercise – Make a list of the things in your life you would like to change. Go ahead, I'll wait here. Please do not come back until you have a minimum of three. No Limit to how many things in your life you want to adjust or remove: Maybe there is an unwanted repeating behavior you would like to stop: Simple, like leaving the dishes in the sink and not rinsing them like your partner would prefer. It only takes seconds to complete. Come on guys. Men not listening enough, Women throwing important things of yours away, (like your Lego Millennium Falcon and beer bottle cap collection from your one month in college) Men not lifting the toilet seat, Men not putting the toilet seat down…

STOP: Wait a minute, we all want to feel equal in a relationship, right? Where is the fair and equal distribution of duties here? …or would that be doody's…doodies? Either way, shouldn't we each pick one? Up or down, it's only fair. You get the first choice. Ah never mind, it's more important for you honey, so I will be cognizant of pee-pee time.

If my toilet etiquette sidebar snagged your attention, and you haven't completed the exercise yet, I apologize. GO! Make your list of habits and behaviors you do not like. Add them to your list of at least 3 things. Do it now please.

Thank you

Chapter 2
Thinking Outside the Box

* * *

What is a Thought?

With a faster-than-normal brain, I have been thinking about thinking and thought for years. This is how I envision the process and how that thought gets formed into words from the eyes of an advanced Improviser. I am not a doctor, but I've played one in a sketch or three. That said, this is my explanation or my interpretation of a typical thought from start to finish:

- First, something happens.
- Then an instant impulse is sent to your BOSS. (we'll get to Him or Her later)
- This spark searches through the pre-existing files and the long-established beliefs you created as a child.
- A file is selected. This file is completely based on past experiences you have associated with whatever influenced the current thought in the first place.
- The next step is not rational or analytical thinking, it is based on RE-action.
- We begin to feel the senses, memories, and feelings that come up for us the moment the current thought arrives. Bam = Emotion.

We usually react based on something pulled from these old tapes and past files. You end up reacting to yesterday's file and the fear of tomorrow's results. This limiting use of your filing system washes away many valuable – natural – instinctive – impulse-driven, actionable thoughts. This process happens in less than a fraction of a millisecond. Improvisational Thinking helps to keep you in the moment, to be present and open.

IT enables us to catch the thought impulse, take a beat to avoid behaving based on the old file, and select an appropriate response or action based on the current experience happening right now. We can easily get caught up in our thoughts. Daydreaming, overthinking, boredom, anger, sadness, etc. There is not much value in getting caught up in those thoughts right now. Change the channel, get present, and refocus on the Now. You can also just think of something or someone else less upsetting or with no clothes on.

Most of this Improvisational Thinking process has developed over 30+ years of improvising and selling it. Throughout my life, I have had many fantastic Mentors. I've also had my share of TorMentors. I prefer the mentors much more.

I've met and spent some time with some of the top thought leaders out there. Dr. Wayne Dyer, Brian Tracy, and Simon Sinek to name a few. One of the most enlightened people I have ever known was Judy Winchel. My father and Judy's husband Danny Winchel were entertainers and besides Barry, they were best friends. Judy was my mother's closest friend too, so they learned a lot from each other.

While my mom shared her Marilynisms with the world, and quite a bit of gas, oh yeah. My mother's farts could've knocked a vulture off a rotting carcass. Judy also gifted me with many of her Judy-isms and a fart, or two too. Over many years and many conversations, Judy's influence and the tools she and my mom gave me, helped me grow mentally and substantially.

Judy taught me how to analyze an upset develop skills and

thought processes to help me master how to deal with my neurodivergent brain and those thoughts that create the upset.

As children, we are not equipped to deal with traumatic incidents or living in crisis. With each unhappy experience, we tend to push it inward to a place where we hide the shame, fears or embarrassment. Unfortunately, we arrest our development at the age this occurs. So as adults, when a similar issue happens your BOSS may find a connection logged to an experience. This triggers the memory. Thoughts, feelings, emotions flow, body sensations, verbal spewing's, and acting out. It's all a reaction and a reminder of that past experience. Upsets are part of the human condition. Being a douchebag doesn't have to be. We all get upset. Everyone wants to be right. Nobody wants to be wrong. Unfortunately, in having to be right, someone or something else has to be wrong. This comes from judgments we made at critical times in our lives. Judging that way since that initial experience stopped us from literally growing up where a particular issue is concerned. But judgments are just thoughts, and every human being thinks and may also judge those who are different.

Growing up, I witnessed a lot of people judging others. Judgments come up for us when we feel we have to be better than someone else, or their stuff might be better than our stuff, so you shit on them or their stuff. Good or bad, right or wrong, even negative and positive when used as a way of being right, is classic judgmental behavior. Envy and jealousy are also natural emotions. The problem with both is this is an unfulfilled desire.

A deep desire to not feel like you're at the back of the line. When these feelings of judgment or envy are rising within you, a sense of being less than, or your stuff is not as cool as their stuff. Therefore, you are not cool. These thoughts can consume you. Judy would say that critical thinking is based on old fears we developed as we were growing up. As children, incidents happened in our lives that made us afraid. And at the bottom of all those incidents are one of several conditions. When we have expectations about the way we want things to be, and they're not happening that way, we set ourselves up for disappointment. When we try to change others to fit our pictures of them, without success, we experience hopelessness and defeat. Conflicts unfold out of a misinterpretation of intentions, responding with Silence, or lying about eating the last Oreo. This is why I founded Comedyation™. We take your conflict and turn it into comedy. We also help those who cannot muster the courage to tell someone something of importance to them without severe anxiety taking over. We also help those who deal with inner self-conflict. Check it out @ comedyation.com

At one point I had an opportunity to buy a brownstone for a fraction of its value. The issue was, it was a total mess. There was going to be a lot of hard work, money, and time. That property would have secured my future and the future of my children... that didn't physically exist yet. If only I had taken the risk. If only I did not let the negative advice, opinions from others, and self-doubt prevent me from pulling the trigger. If only I didn't get the RV and build that meth lab with Jessie. Oh, wait, no. That was Breaking Bad.

When I recently took a look at that property on Zillow and saw its current value, I was shocked, I was embarrassed and I was angry. I blamed myself for listening to everyone else back then and not believing in my gut instincts.

When we allow others to talk us out of doing something we want to do, we feel weaker. Yes, sometimes taking their advice is a good idea. No Adam, don't go skinny dipping in your soon-to-be in-law's jacuzzi. Especially during her mom's Mahjong game. Gladys will never be the same. When we truly believe it is the right thing to do for ourselves, but still surrender our choice to somebody else we'll usually be upset, probably blame them and become bitter and frustrated, just reinforcing the self-doubt and increasing self-abuse. When we hold back from speaking our truth, because we are afraid, because we think we might hurt someone, or because we have horrible limburger breath, our effective communication skills shut down. When we get lost in our heads, we internalize resentment, we punish ourselves and others when we really don't deserve it, and at that point upsets are inevitable.

When we're aware of these conditions and process the thought intelligently…every time we become upset, we can identify what we really want and need at that moment.

We can deal with the upset responsibly. And the beauty is, we have the power to stop ourselves anywhere in the process. No one has the power to upset us unless we allow them to. Even ourselves.

Upsets start with a thought connected to a past experience. All senses, feelings, and emotions follow. There is a process to find helpful solutions to an upset. Through practicing conscious commitment, heightened awareness and first taking responsibility for creating my upset, I learned to stop myself from reacting, emotionally, physically, and neurologically…Most of the time. Practice truly does help.

After a time, I was able to stop myself anywhere in the process, from the moment of thought, through the feelings, emotions, body sensations, and even in the middle of flipping out. I can now take a moment to respond, question what comes up, evaluate the validity and take the appropriate action at any given moment during said flip out. Instead of seeing things through the eyes of an adult, we're still being influenced by the child that lives inside us. I am not saying I don't ever lose my shit; I do. I just don't allow it to stay and hang around. It's gotta go. Flush.

Upsets occur when we are reminded of those unpleasant

childhood or teenage memories. Like the wedgie Scott Makowski gave you in third grade, or the time Lisa Jordan said she would go with you to the dance and then ended up going with Marc Brady who always had horrible breath and never combed his hair, or as simple as the time the rainbow sprinkled scoop fell of off your cone. The upset doesn't always have to happen. When we listen to and nurture that inner child, we can protect ourselves by refusing to give in to the bullshit. We can choose an appropriate adult response. By acknowledging "what's just happened", understanding it is what it is and other than your own choices leave you powerless. When this happens, I say, "I'm sorry" and forgive myself and others. A simple apology can accomplish amazing results.

It doesn't matter how upset we are, it's how we handle it and how fast we recover that makes the difference. When we step away from our inner critical thinking and self-doubt built on yesterday's experiences, we flourish. When we observe and speak the truth without judgment, we begin to heal those old wounds seeded in our childhood memories leaving us free to experience our own value and self-worth. With practice we discover the source of our true core beliefs and issues, we can test, clear, reprogram, and re-pattern any unnecessary, unworkable, unfriendly thoughts and inappropriate emotionally driven behaviors that kept us from experiencing the true beauty of our authentic Selves.

When upsets happen around us, we can behave like a three-year-old who does not want to wear pants (that's my go-to), or we can act like the healthy grown-ups we are, and be there to support and assist those we love and care about, making it easier for them to love and care about you.

Life's all about how you handle curveballs, and ditching that inner critic lets you flourish by embracing truth without judgment and healing old wounds. With practice, uncovering the roots of your beliefs allows you to kick out unfriendly thoughts and drop emotionally wonky behaviors. Now, fear on the other hand is that party crasher trying to censor your creative thoughts, but remember, you're the captain of your thoughts. Don't let fear be the bouncer.

Fear Shall Not Deny Me

Fear Censors Creative Thought. Fear has a way of creeping into our thoughts and consuming the moment. You have no power over the initial instinctual "Red Alert" signal that accompanies fear.

Here is a fact: YOU Control Your Thoughts, Your Thoughts DO NOT Control You. Too often people with great creativity and intuitive thinking come up with a great idea and it stays an idea. If you truly believe your idea is worthy of the masses, it should be pursued. Go for it! Sometimes taking the risk is what delivers the reward.

Unfortunately, for the many "ideas" formulated in the mind, many go nowhere. The fear of risk outweighs the thoughts of success. Why would we not take the risk? The reasons will vary. Here is an example of a good reason.

You can see a bear eating your steak dinner. You do not want the bear to eat your dinner. Do you risk going out there and telling the bear to go away? Or, do you let the bear eat your meat? It's rhetorical.

Time Traveling' Exercise

The human brain…your virtual life library…your thinking machine…a time machine able to travel backward through time…or create and imagine the future. You can go anywhere in a split second. Let's try this simple exercise for a moment just for you to personally solidify what I mean by this. With your eyes closed, let's go back to the first memory you have. You got it? Yup, that one. Now move to around 13 … then up to another clear happy memory from your past. Would you be surprised to know that the brain waves that are creating the memory, are nearly identical to the actual live recording? It is as if you are truly there. You cannot touch it, but you can bring up the feelings that existed at the time your database recorded it.

Now let's go into the future. It's your future, 1st Rule: Visualize, but only using your positive imagination. You are happy with this. Think fast!

Chapter 3
Start Right Now You're Already Here

* * *

Start Right now?

In this chapter, we'll explore how embracing your true self, facing challenges head-on, trusting your instincts, and understanding the power of your own story can make you a more agile, effective, and enjoyable salesperson. Welcome to the journey of becoming a master of sales with the power to induce smiles!

You are perfect exactly the way you are. If not, you'd be something else. Maybe a shoe, or a potato, or a discarded toenail? You know, that one big toe toenail that when clipped, flew away never to be seen again. That is until your wife finds it by stepping on the now dangerous shard. As you are reading this, I am guessing you are not a discarded toenail. They can't read.

You are exactly who you are supposed to be, today. This does not mean you can't be or do something else tomorrow. Today I am just a little overweight. I used to be a lot overweight. As I write this, I am currently 168 lbs. lighter than I was a few years ago. This is a major achievement for me that I must stay vigilant or it will all return with a vengeance. Will I still be in shape when you read this, I don't know…but I don't think about it. I know I am still a bit overweight. Tomorrow, I will still be overweight. By following LARRY (I'll introduce you to him shortly), I won't be, I only have to deal with today. Right now. I can choose to fixate on this unpleasant weighted fact or continue to live my life and focus on what I can do today to better myself. Just today. This moment. I don't get lost in fantasy land. Stay present. Be you. You are perfect.

Luckily, I was given the gift of being able to communicate my thoughts in a way that is both kind and frank. Serious, but funny. Tell true stories or I make them up…its Acting. Speaking and performing have gotten me far in life. Deep down, I feel I am supposed to assist others and help them to break their limiting beliefs, knock down their barriers and eliminate their excuses. To JUST GO FOR IT…whatever their "IT" is.

Turn on Your Switch!

For years…no decades, I led a life that did not support a healthy lifestyle. There are still moments, even days where I don't. It was as if my common sense left the building and the ability to make choices that were in my best interest was asleep. Consistently.

When you're conscious, you do not ignore the growth and reach 424 lbs. I lived in the darkness that was my inner mind. There was nothing of value coming my way. I was not mindful, my mind was full of regrets, anxiety, self-doubt, and low self-worth.

I remember my mother or her friend Judy using the term "Today is the first day of the rest of your life". I always liked the idea of being able to instantly make a change. In my imagination, I visualized this as a light switch. When it's off, it's dark. When the switch is on, there is light. It's interesting how those two terms beyond their literal definitions also seem to cover a state of being. One positive, one negative.

All it takes is making a true decision. The word decision comes from the Latin meaning "To cut off." A friend once gave me his brilliant definition of a true decision. It's like crossing the bridge and blowing it up behind you. Making it clear there is no going back. I like that one. It took me turning my switch back on, consciously paying attention to what was happening right now, and taking accountability for my words and my actions. Once all of the bullshit exited my schedule, the wind was at my back! Is today the first day of the rest of your life? Turn your switch on and see.

Stay Focused on the Now: Change Now

Improvisational Thinking is a helpful way/skill/trait to assist you in times of change and unforeseen obstacles. Staying in the moment keeps you Sharper, and gives you Higher Performance, Confidence, Motivation, Acceptance, and Teamwork. Letting go of the need for and attachment to status and ego. Sometimes it is difficult to believe your best days are ahead of you. I promise change will come easier to those who follow the focused path

The Now is Where It All Happens

If you are focused on what is happening in front of you. If you are truly looking, listening, and taking it all in, you will be better at downloading input. You will comprehend much more, learn much more, and file that information to your memory bank. Bank each of the experiences you enjoy. Bank the characters you meet. Remember stinky Bob? Suzie with the hairy arms and bad teeth and your neighbor, creepy Mr. Ploop? File it all away and trust that when a particular piece contained in one of the billions of files is needed, your mind will instantly pop a few options up for you. Trusting that process is key. This is how an Improviser or Comedian can select a funnier word or sentence than the average person. Make a facial reaction, or reference the odd bit.

Happiness

"Happiness is locked out when we choose to allow our negative thoughts to control us." Why do we do what we do? For me. everything I do in my working life comes down to one thing. "Will this make me happy? Can I find passion in this?" If the answer is no, I don't do it...Unless my wife says so. Money can help to get you more stuff and yes money is a great tool to help get things done, but the evidence is in. Money cannot and will not buy you happiness. On the other hand, your happiness can attract a lot more than money.

The best way for me to achieve this state of happiness is to stay in the present. By staying in the moment and getting out of my head, I find myself in a much better mood, I get more accomplished in less time and one great added byproduct is...I often find my happiness level is infectious.

Remember what I said earlier? YOU Control Your Thoughts, Your Thoughts DO NOT Control You. Too often our inner thoughts get squashed down and wiped away due to our own self-judgment. The goal is to help you and your business, team, family, friends and any other accomplices in your life to go to war with these negative thoughts and win the battle every time! Self-doubt can go f...or a swim! Limiting yourself ends today. Self-limitations are gone! Well, except for eating three pizzas.

Isn't happiness what we all strive for? Do you want to be happier more often? Improvisational Thinking is a great additional tool to add to your happiness toolbox!

Now you can increase those moments of happiness substantially with this fun new ability to stay consciously aware in the present and become a more mindful human being.

Quick wit, brain-twisting games are a fun way to train your mind to work faster and more efficiently. These mind workouts are better and a lot more fun than doing the New York Times Crossword Puzzle, Sudoku, or Wordle. Having improv skills in your pocket can help keep you from missing out on these important happy moments, become the party starter, or deliver the speech or presentation you always avoided.

Experience more of your own life as it happens. Everyone loves to play games. These games have no pieces to lose, no spinners or dice. Improv games are a great way to spend family time. Being present. Stop thinking and start being!

Why don't more people try improv? Because they are afraid to look silly, they are shy, they believe you have to think faster than they can't and they don't think they are funny. Instead of pleasure, they associate fear and pain.

Improvising is pure freedom. Freedom keeps us happier. There is no plan, it is acting in the moment without knowing, confident in your ability, and it's that simple. Each of us is improving every day by experiencing and responding in the moment. Being in the moment is different than living in the moment. I am not talking about jumping out of a plane, bungee jumping, or partying till you pass out. I am talking about being present.

People get caught up in their fantasy world within their heads. Their thoughts are consumed with resentment, regrets, and maybe even remorse for yesterday's past. Or they get caught up in the Fear, Anxiety, and Anticipation of an unknown tomorrow. Right now, Yesterday's and Tomorrow's are nothing more than fantasy. Now is what matters for your state of mind.

I want to introduce you to the magic of Improvisational Thinking by teaching you a few exercises and fun games. I have trained and worked with people of all ages and from all walks of life. Kids to Senior Citizens and everyone in between. From CEOs to the

Janitor. To us, it's all the same. Happiness is not a destination.

Through innovative, thought-provoking, mind training, you can learn to use the skills and core principles of Improvisation. Your comfort level will be raised, your ability to respond will increase, and you will take more risks and challenge the status quo.

You will find yourself smiling more often and a great byproduct of this training…your humorous side will be revealed more often than your grumpy side. If you want to enjoy your family time, be happier, to remain clear and conscious, Do the exercises and play the games I've shared here. I promise you will notice you are happier as days go by.

Happiness is not a location you can drive to. It is a state of mind. We simply want more of those moments of happiness. We seek it out in so many ways. Some methods are not very healthy for our mental health. From Drugs to Food, Gambling, or even Sex.

It's not like you can schedule a moment of happiness. That just doesn't happen.

"Sorry, Bob. I cannot make that meeting tomorrow. I have happiness scheduled at 11:15."

Happiness is unannounced. Like a sneeze or a laugh, happiness is an involuntary physical, sensual, visual, and mental reaction filled with positive emotions and whatever nice feelings come up.

One of my happy places is watching others perform. I go to concerts with my son, shows with my daughter, and school sports events with my youngest. My Mom and Dad always took me to Broadway to see Plays and Musicals. We even saw movies when they still played at Radio City Music Hall.

One happy night, I was in my late 30s when I went to see Oklahoma. I had just finished shooting a fun Star Wars

Mockumentary on Episode One. I worked with a brilliantly funny and talented comedic actor named, Aasif Mandvi. He is on CBS' Evil, the Daily Show, and in the movie Analyze This, where he had the best scene in the film; he almost got whacked after telling DeNiro he was having a Panic Attack...I digress...again.

Aasif was performing that night as Ali Hakim the Persian peddler. His role was very short; only two scenes, maybe 10 minutes total. My wife and I both agreed, he almost stole the show. I said to my wife. I think I may be able to pull off a role like that someday, but I quickly let that idea go. Who am I kidding? I've never taken an acting class or been in a play or musical in my life. I was an improv/stand-up comic that got one commercial and jumped in the pool from there. Was my being on Broadway achievable? Ironically, the actor cast in the main role of Curly that day would come into play later and...Wait...I'm getting ahead of myself.

"To think? Or...not to think? That is the question!"
- NOT William Shakespeare

Happiness

By Adam Sietz 6/13/2010

Happiness is where you'll find it
It could be right under your shoe
If you're still looking outward for happiness
It might just avoid finding you
Happiness is not a location
It's not in a place you can go
You cannot arrive at happiness
But there is one thing you should know
Happiness is in all the little things
It comes and it goes as it pleases
I once felt happiness sweep over me
Just after 3 glorious sneezes
Happiness surrounds my children
It makes an appearance every day
The children can see it, because they believe it
When you look at their faces at play
You marry your love you feel happiness
Your baby is born you feel happiness
You get a great haircut you feel happiness
But if it's a bad one well that's nappy-ness
It won't be found near your ego
Or your jealousy or your hate
But you taste it just a little bit
On the top of warm pie on your plate
When you realize you are loved
You are sure to find some happiness
And if you lose the ones you love
It's their happiness that you miss
When you are content with who you are
Even when life doesn't seem fair
You'll see that happiness surrounds you
And you will find it everywhere

Act 2:
Laughs and Longevity:
Succeeding in Relationships and
Business with I.T.

Chapter 4
Improvisational Thinking

* * *

The Invitation

When we approach the conclusion of this book, I extend a heartfelt invitation to you. The information within these pages is not meant to be merely absorbed; it's meant to be lived and put into action. It's an invitation to embrace Improvisational Thinking as a powerful tool in your professional arsenal, to break free from shyness, and to elevate your skills in communicating, selling, and business.

Remember that the journey you are embarking on is not just about learning techniques or acquiring skills; it's about transforming yourself into a more confident, adaptable, and effective professional. Improvisational Thinking is not just a tool; it's a mindset, a way of approaching the world with openness, flexibility, and creativity.

So, my friend, with an open heart and an eager mind, grab the popcorn and let's dive into the world of Improvisational Thinking. Let's discover how it can revolutionize your approach to daily life, business, and sales. Together, we'll unlock the incredible potential that already lies within you.

Seriously. It's in there, you may just be in its way. Get out your way. Once I did? Wooo! Health, Wealth, and now more Stealth are my adjectives. Beats the heck out of Fat, Uncomfortable, and quite possibly smelly. Ewww.

Now Let Go and Just Be!

Unleashing your Inner Improviser

Now, you might think that improvisation is reserved for musicians, comedians, and bad actors. Well, think again. It's a skill that anyone can and should develop, including you. It's a skill that can change the way you approach thinking about every aspect of your personal and professional life. You already improvise daily. Conversations are Improvised. Think about it. You speak, they reply. You speak again, not knowing what you were going to say moments before those words came out of your mouth.

In the following pages, I'll share stories of hope and inspiration, a wide range of what I believe are helpful thoughts, and maybe a fart joke. Someone else may disagree with me on certain topics, I am completely okay with that, I may not agree with them either but...they still get a big hug too!

Improvisational Thinking exercises and techniques will help you to tap into your inner lexicon of obscured encyclopedic knowledge logged into one of the billions of files you already have stored somewhere in your brain. These games, practices, and exercises are not just about boosting your confidence; they're about enhancing your ability to concentrate, communicate, and collaborate. To make quick decisions more clearly, confidently, and creatively—skills essential in the world of life and in business.

I.T. (No not that IT) - Improvisational Thinking

In the world of sales, there's a secret weapon that can help you achieve unscripted success: IT = Improvisational Thinking.

By getting out of your head, and staying focused on the Now, we leave less room for our mind to get stuck in the future or the past.

Fear and anxiety of possible outcomes or the regret and upset based on yesterday or moments ago are presently all pure fantasy. FANTASY. When we are truly in the moment, we can be ourselves. Your brain can improvise in any given situation and save the day. It can pull up needed information in a fraction of a second. It can give you a visual of that sexy person naked as if you were there…Ok some computer systems can do that, but they are not connected to beautiful brown eyes and a new comfy pair of Air Jordan 1's. Here is a good example of the simplest variety of why your brain is tops.

YOU: A large cup of coffee spills all over you.

COMPUTER: A large cup of coffee spills all over… it.

YOU: Immediately grab a towel and dry yourself off.

COMPUTER: Just sits there…and within moments…it is fried.

- Improvisational Thinking helps me/us to utilize thought in a positive, innovative, creative, passionate, humorous,and many other ways…with colorful adjectives to describe its effect and enhanced function ability when put into use.
- Improvisational Thinking could be summed up as TRUE EXPERIENCE
- Improvisational Thinking is staying in the moment and being present.
- Improvisational Thinking doesn't care about yesterday's regrets.
- Improvisational Thinking does not care about fear of tomorrow's unknowable outcomes.
- Improvisational Thinking unleashes humor
- Humor unleashes smiles and laughter
- Smiles and Laughter equals Happiness.
- Happiness surrounds us
- Happiness Rules!

- Happiness is there for the taking.
- Happiness is not a location. It is not an attainable goal...It just is.
- Being in a state of Happiness (more often than not) is all that we really want from life. It's the bottom line of what drives us. Does that make sense? Yes, it does!

Improvisational Thinking delivers benefits including educational, business, and successful life factors including (but not limited to) the following:

Importance of Eye Contact
Public Speaking
Extreme Concentration
Focused and Structured Communication
Team Work
Listening Skills
Creative Thinking
Team Bonding
Give and Take
Making Strong Choices
Commitment
Risk Taking
Dealing with Adversity
Inner Beliefs Change
Acceptance
Exploring
Feelings and Emotions
Intuition
Inclusion of All
Better Collaboration

Get With IT:

1. Confidence in yourself and your abilities.
2. Improvisers develop richer communicative

relationships due to being our authentic selves.

3. Developing a Stronger Humorous Presentation
4. Stronger Presence and Performance Skills.
5. Become a better storyteller. Share Richer Fuller's Sensory experiences.
6. Learn to trust your gut instincts and act on them without self-judgment.
7. Improve your ability to respond to the unexpected.
8. Increased and Enhanced Mental Agility.
9. Ability to uncover and inject humor in the moment.
10. You find the humor in everyday events.
11. Practiced improvisational techniques can de-stress and create a relaxed state.
12. The ability to be comfortably at ease dealing with the unplanned events.
13. You will rule the day more often and feel like the King of your universe!

5 Simple Rules of Improvisation

Rule #1: YES, AND! Stop saying NO so quickly. Instead, think "YES, AND". This concept helps to lay the foundation of Improv. This fundamental formula of starting with a Yes will often help to open up and reveal useful information for you. For me, by always saying yes at first, I find it allows me to take time to accumulate more valuable information to make a thoughtful, in-depth decision.

Nobody said I couldn't change my mind and politely say No at a later junction.

By getting into the habit of saying Yes, now and then building on the initial thought by adding…AND…I have been, and you will be blessed to witness true unleashed innovation and creativity thrive! Say yes to joining your friends for the concert, say yes to getting on that roller coaster. Say yes to that Hawaiian-style pizza with ham and pineapple you have refused to even try (surprisingly it doesn't suck). I once said yes to ordering Rooster Chips. Thinking they were chicken nuggets, I ate a few. They were not bad, but after the third bite, I found out what Rooster Chips are. Use your imagination.

Rule #2: <u>LISTEN FIRST THEN THINK</u> As you already know, focused listening is so important. If you are busy thinking about what you want to say next or what you forgot to say before, you cannot concentrate on the input coming at you. Listen first, get where others are coming from before you speak.

Rule #3: <u>AVOID ASKING QUESTIONS</u> In the business world and in life, when we take time to ask a lot of questions, we often end up making the other participant(s) do all of the work. I am not saying to ask no questions, just be conscious of how you can make statements instead. How YOU can frame your statement in a way that covers your intended goals. "Ok I will drive, but you're buying". You may also find when someone asks you a question and you instantly know if you answer the question truthfully as asked, it can hurt - not only to help your cause, you can find ways to reframe the answer to fit your needs. Many times, this maneuver fulfills the need of the questioner without having to be untruthful. "How do I look in this dress?" Yes, "You look beautiful" is the correct answer when your wife or girlfriend asks that question. But if you are a friend, you can reframe it to get things to kindly go in the direction you want them to go. "I saw another one and I believe you will look nice in that dress more, and the style is so much more you!

Rule #4: <u>EYE CONTACT & PAY ATTENTION</u> Focused attention is hard to keep. Distractions can take you off the track and out of the game. Like when you are up at bat, and a beautiful girl is walking into the stands, it's never a good idea to lose focus to look at her. If you do, know that she may pay attention to your private parts…when the baseball hits you in the nuts. Body language or just a simple look on someone's face can instantly communicate a feeling of like or dislike. Even when you are on the telephone, you can sense and pick up on the cues, clues, and the tone and or demeanor of the other person. Stay conscious and focused, look people directly in the eyes, and be aware of the offers and opportunities surrounding you in the moment.

Rule #5: ADD INFORMATION When you begin to "Yes and…" in your life, you are adding more information to the conversation. You are building on the initial jump-off point. The more information entering your BOSS, or info you are putting out there for someone else to upload into their BOSS, the more associations and connections open up leading to the connection found in the ocean of knowledge already stored in our BOSS.

The better you stay current and know who is involved, what is happening, and where you wish to end up, the better you truly get to know clients. Always keep in touch with all clients. Check-in to see how they are doing. While you are at it, ASK if there is anything new or anything you can do to be of service. You are not selling, you are only reconnecting and sending best wishes. You will be shocked to see how many of those pure reconnecting calls lead to deals.

Improvisers become less anxious. We stop focusing our thoughts on the negative and leave the stressors behind. We won't allow ourselves to be terrorized by self-induced pressure. We embrace whatever comes (or run away faster). We become more proactive, and more organized and take more self-accountability for our words and actions. We give more than we take.

Reframing

Improvisers have this innate ability to reframe situations

positively, without too much attachment to the old way of doing it. "Wait! What? I'll have to lose my left leg?! Ouch. Well, I guess that's one less shoe I'll have to buy for life, Score!" This is a terrific skill for adapting to any changes in life. We become more comfortable being able to Let Go and Just Be. If you live without putting any bullshit out of your mouth or bullshitting yourself. Live truthfully, your authenticity will shine and you will be establishing true credibility and a comfortable rapport with every interaction.

For example, a prospect says no. Do not let go just yet. Politely ask for help here. "Before I let you go, may I please get some feedback? It will help me understand your objection and grow as I go. Would you help me?" Sometimes, they will not give you the time to share any of your info. You just get a no. CLICK! (or if you're lucky, a no…thank you). Onto the next.

A higher percentage than you would think will want to help someone who ASKS them for it. You do have to ask for it.

Once you know the objection you can directly address their concerns. Let them know you were listening. Let them know their objections are valid and understandable, "…and 'perhaps it's because I didn't tell you…blah blah blah. Does this make you more comfortable? Are there any other questions or concerns I can relieve you of? Would like a lollipop? Or would you like to…

   A. *Use the next 2 minutes to curse at me and berate me?"*
   B. *Tell Hanibal to beat me for two minutes. To pay for the two minutes of your life you can never get back?*
   C. *Tell me when I should follow up. Can I call you on August 12th? Or, can I count you in already? A contract? Sure, Great!*

Once you can get them to share their reason behind the "No", start reframing your question. You will still need to dance around the objections by emphasizing the benefits and highlighting the unique value you're delivering. Share some similar case studies, and suggest alternative options that may better fit their needs. It is a bit different today than it was when I was gunning every day on the telephone. Today, a salesman has many more tools to find new prospects. From lead generation to SEO, and Google. To detailed lists and let's not forget AI. Ha! I used a tickler file.

That was a real file drawer with the entire calendar broken down into 12 folders. One for each month of the year. In the current month, there were 31 date cards. Each month you would move the date cards into the next month's file and divvy up all that month's call sheets. These sheets included any bit of information I could mine, every note I had written down along with exact dates to call; these were dates that were ASKED for, and freely given by the prospective client. That client and newest phone friend will be looking forward to speaking to you again.

Selling is not just about getting that money; it's about building trust with your new partner. It is about you joining their project, or you sharing your viewpoint in a nice conversation between new friends. Who knows, it may end up with a $weet ending. Cha-ching

Nobody likes to be sold. They do like to buy things they want. The key is to show them why they would want what you're selling, without over-selling.

Harvard University's Stress and Development lab had this to say:

Positive Reframing and Examining of the Evidence

Two types of reappraisal that are particularly effective are **positive reframing** and **examining the evidence**.

Positive reframing involves thinking about a negative or challenging situation in a more positive way. This could involve thinking about a benefit or upside to a negative situation that you had not considered. Alternatively, it can involve identifying a lesson to be learned from a difficult situation. Finding something to be grateful about in a challenging situation is a type of positive reappraisal. For example, after a break-up you could think about the opportunities to meet new people, the things you learned from the relationship, and the gratitude you feel for the time you spent with the person.

Examining the evidence involves weighing the evidence for your interpretation of a situation. This involves examining the assumptions you are making about how other people are thinking, feeling, or likely to behave. You might evaluate how likely it is that a negative outcome occurs, think about how often a negative outcome has happened in the past in a similar situation, or think about what the worst possible outcome is (and whether it is likely to happen), and whether you could handle if it did happen. You can also ask yourself: "What is the evidence that this outcome will happen?" For example, after performing poorly on an assignment and worrying about the consequences on your GPA, you can think about other assignments you have done well on in the past, the likelihood that you will be able to do well on the next assignment, and whether you could handle getting a lower grade than you wanted if it did happen.

Other strategies for reappraisal include reminding yourself that thoughts aren't facts, identifying **extreme language** (e.g., I will always feel this way; things will never get better) and rephrasing with less extreme words, questioning the **assumptions or biases** that led to your interpretation, and taking on **someone else's perspective**. (e.g., if you told someone else about the situation, would they interpret it the same way?)

Sometimes the first way we reappraise a situation won't stick, and that's okay. It's important to try to think about situation flexibly in different ways until you land on an interpretation that feels right to you. This is not always going to be the most positive interpretation!

Changing the Status Quo

It was 2011. We were bidding for a nice writing project. This was a spin-off from an internationally known animated series. Other companies were competing with us for the project.

I had met the CEO of a giant animation firm at either NATPE, Mipcom, or the Kidscreen convention, but I did not know if we made a good enough impression for him to include us in the bid. When I reconnected with the CEO, he requested some samples. Knowing that we were up against some extremely talented individuals, I decided to break with the status quo.

"I'm sorry, but we don't do that."

The look on his face was priceless. Seeing the confusion, I explained: "We do not like sending samples of work that was done previously. What we would like to do is give you some fresh, new writing samples that are constructed specifically for your project. Based on the show's bible (the complete file of information available on the show), we will customize the samples we would deliver to you, all for the whopping price of…$0.00."

These personally customized scenes will be written by multiple different writers. We had a strong group of writers. Some had great CVs. Some had written for SNL, the Daily Show, Conan, and Letterman. We also had first time newcomers with no resume at all, but have proven extremely talented. To keep the process fair for all of our writers submitting their samples, we submitted them all anonymously. Writer A, B, C, etc. We wanted to stand out. My confidence was very strong in the belief that he could not possibly hate all of the samples and refuse them all. It was like handing him a menu from Baskin-Robbins. He received a variety of 31 different flavors. Okay, maybe it was eight, but still, you get the point.

This show is very important to him. It's like a very popular dish that he has created, but we must show him that we can cook it as good as anyone out there, or better.

In the end, he liked two of the eight writers we submitted. We wrote half of the first season while his writing staff wrote the other half. This was a risky maneuver, as we all put in our time for no compensation to validate our quality and value. This project was very fruitful. This model has worked well over and over again.

Chapter 5
Improvisational Thinking in Relationships

* * *

Stop Competing…With yourself!

Winning! I've never been one for competition. That said, if I am involved in a competition, you bet your ass I wanna win. I have met many people who always seem to compete with everyone. We spoke about Ego and Status, and we may have also heard the saying: "The only competition you can lose is one you choose to participate in". I am not saying competition is not good. I lived for Little League, so much so I knew I could never be my son's coach. I could assist but keeping my mouth shut would have been virtually impossible. Competition can bring the worst out of us. I knew my limits as I knew this to be true. The New York Giants killed my father. They were not very good at the time and fumbled away one too many.

I saw some of the most ridiculous examples of unnecessary competition when I was 10. Just one month after my mom surprised my father for his 40th birthday by buying him a bright orange Corvette Stingray, our next-door neighbor bought a little Red Corvette and completely went way overboard pimping it out with Von Dutch pinstriping on steroids. I also remember a stupid example of a ridiculous competition. I was at a high school party, and there was a keg of beer and a fierce game of quarters.

If you don't know what quarters is, it is a game where you fill a small glass with some beer. People then take turns trying to bounce a quarter into the glass. If you sink it, you get to pick who drinks it. I was OK at this game, but I knew when to bow out. Some people would stay in until someone had to carry them home. That is if they haven't thrown up all over themselves. At that point, they were on their own.

In a work setting, competing with each other can be healthy in a sales competition. It doesn't have to be. Everyone has to get their job done, meet their quota, and deliver to keep their position and bring home the bacon.

As long as you stay, focused, and conscious of what you need to do for yourself. If you're kicking a$$ daily, who do you need to compete with? Being driven to succeed is healthy, but your success does not always have to mean someone else's failure. There doesn't always have to be a winner and a loser. Sometimes both…Quite often both, lose because the competition takes over. Teamwork evaporates if the teammates compete with each other. With improvisational thinking, you enjoy making your partners look good.

You've seen it, two people battle it out against each other. While they consume themselves with having to beat the other, a dark horse comes from behind and takes the crown.

I never liked the saying "You're only competing against yourself". Why do that? Why would I make myself my own opponent? Do you want to beat yourself? Not me. I just choose to take actionable accountability. Remain consistent and believe in yourself and the skills you know to empower yourSELF every day. A bad day will pop up, so choose to stay on track. Don't allow your inner critic to throw you off your game. Self-doubt has no place in your life anymore. You are who you are. Today is the best you, you could be.Tomorrow if you wanna be better…be better. Stop competing withyourself, and join the team. Your team.

Your Ego is Unattractive

I find people who have big egos…people who are constantly seeking Status…extremely Unattractive.

"Get any likes?" "Wow! Look how many more followers I have than you!" "Ratio!"

In the business I'm in, I should have a social presence, but as of this moment, squat. It's never been that important. Getting likes? After wanting to be liked in high school, I never even gave the idea of getting "Likes" a thought.

Most of the Social Posting I've seen is often filled with filtered or enhanced photos. They post and show only the selected Grade A filtered photos, and life events. I see a lot of people brag about their new stuff or the exotic places they are vacationing. Never from the toilet bowl they were sitting on when they typed the post.

Nobody posts things like…

"Wozers! I have diarrhea!"
"My kid got arrested last night"
"I hate my brother's children. Little Trolls"

My niece had her pictures stolen and used on accounts made by a Catfish. It seems kind of creepy having tons of followers seeking your attention. To be popular or gain likes is just not something I care about. You shouldn't either. But, be careful what you wish for. Ego doesn't pay our bills.

Pitfalls of Status

In improvisational Comedy, Status, and Ego only get in the way. Let go of your ego and forget about any need or desire for Status!

In my personal opinion, both are pure fantasy! Both are worthless to your soul.

Status seeking is an extrinsic self-centered behavior. Yes, it is a normal occurrence in the natural world. But I believe status does absolutely nothing for us, other than help to stroke our weak unattractive egos!

In the past, status was based on what you do or what you have done or contributed. Now, it is based on what and how much you have, $ and your possessions. Do not get me wrong, a shiny new convertible Corvette and a wife happily covered in diamonds is OK. It just is not important to the rest of the world. Now on the other hand, walking in off the street and noticing people whisper about who you are or getting a table for seven at Peter Luger Steakhouse when they claim to have no tables until June…well that doesn't suck.

If someone else chooses or wants to give you status for some silly reason of their own accord (you have money, a cool car, a beautiful face or body, your job description has you signing autographs, etc.) Go right ahead, and capitalize! And then, enjoy the Porterhouse!

"My house is the Best" … "My Dad drives a Lambroghini" … "My dad drives a beat-up minivan…with white duct tape…covering a crack on the front end."

That last kid …was mine. I will drive Sienna and love her until she dies.

Like my 12-year-old Minivan, YOU are perfect exactly the way you are! You do not need things to prove it. You exist for a reason. We are all uniquely different. Yes, some have more than others, but like I said, having more doesn't bring us happiness.

Show offs brag and show off to gain status and stroke their ego. Some people label others with lower status. They choose to treat those who are different from them horribly. Stories like this next one can be seen in all age groups. It is just a little more covert and not out in the open.

At some point, you've all probably witnessed someone act like an asshole…or just mean. Maybe, one time you may have even participated. Do you have a little brother or sister? Or…you ARE the little brother or sister? I guess, for me, it started there. I was the baby. I held the lowest position in the well-established status order within the sibling structure.

Maybe you or someone close to you have been the target or witnessed that kind of unkind mean-ness. What do they do? What do you do? Just have to deal with it…or fight? Even within friend groups, someone gets picked on more than the rest. It's a natural animal instinct. A pecking order. Who is the most Dominant? BARK, BARK, BARK!

We are Civilized…Animals. A lot of people will sit there, and watch that behavior happen. Not wanting to bring attention to themselves, they…say…nothing.

People make the clear choice to say or do something that may make someone else feel bad to make themselves feel good or to get a laugh and gain status points. It is NOT at all Cool, it's Cruel. I'll repeat, getting a laugh at the expense of another is weak-minded, mean and douchey. You see we're at times unconscious of how damaging simple words or actions we say or do can be. The words come out of our mouths, and they cut. We walk away…it's done…minimal effect on us. Not to the other person. I'm a baby brother. Sticks and Stones? Forget that. I can tell you from experience. Words can harm you…mentally. Punching someone can cause them physical pain, give them boo-boos, and affect their physical health. A sharply worded jab can also cause physical pain. Pain that lingers and affects mental health. Spewing harmful words will not harm you, but those words can leave a lifetime memory that sucks, served up to another, maybe your little brother or someone you call a friend?

Seeking Status, No. Given Status, Yes!

The first time I felt my status was elevated was when I was a 21-year-old P.A. (Production Assistant) for the NY Mets and Channel 9. I was a Piss Ant, a GoFor. "Hey you, Go for this. Yo, Go for that". But I had my first TV credit. People I never spoke to in my life would come up to me like we were best friends.

"Hey guy, I saw your name on TV!"

Then I started doing national commercials and some major TV Shows. Cool huh?

Getting stopped on the street and being recognized was cool. A definite stroke to my ego. I cannot tell you how many times I was stopped…

"Oh Hey! You're that Guy! You Know the Guy from That thing!"

OR

"Do I know you?"

I thought I wanted fame and celebrity until I got a little taste of it. Just a nibble.

I did my first movie. Then a TV Show. Then a national commercial campaign pushing Scrubbing Bubbles Toilet Wipes! I was treated differently. "I saw you on the Chris Rock Show on the TV", "Weren't you on Chappelle Show", "I saw you at the Comic Strip Live", "I saw you in that commercial…Can you wipe my butt?"

Witnessing the side effects of real fame…at the highest level. While working with some well-known performers, actors, or musicians that have gained Celebrity Level Status. They cannot walk a half block without being molested for an autograph or "Can We Take a Selfie?" Their Privacy doesn't exist and they all hate that part of their work.

If someone gives you status, go ahead and capitalize.

Building True Bonds

One of the most significant benefits of incorporating Improvisational Thinking into your daily and professional life. is the ability to build genuine connections. In an era where authenticity is highly valued, virtual employees have a difficult time socializing with their peers. So can those working six feet away from each other. Little kids make friends easily. "Hey, I have a ball. Wanna Play?" "Sure, okay!" and off they go. When we play well with others, team culture, collaboration, and helpful support become easier. So do new clients, new people, and nice profit$.

Later you will read about it and I will repeat it again and again. Taking the expressway may get you there, but the scenic route will be much more enjoyable. Take the scenic route when starting a new relationship. This is the way to find community and truly make lasting mutually beneficial connections.

Whistling with Woody

"Cut! OK let's take 30 minutes so we could set up the next shot". Wow, that wasn't as hard as I thought, that was easy. I walked over to the Craft services table to see what kind of Nibblies they have. I heard a whistle. It was a familiar tune. It took a moment, but I recognized it as "Pennies from Heaven ". I wasn't sure who was whistling, but as someone who has been paid to whistle, I thought, I have the chops to join in. So, I did. I chose to do a harmony on the whistle and jazz it up. As I walked past the lights, I saw the person whistling with me. It was the director himself, Woody Allen. He smiled and we finished the song. This was the 90's. It all happened before the news of his alleged creepiness was known.

Now at the time you should know, this man was one of the most recognized directors in all of film. Most actors could only dream of being selected to portray one of his characters. Oh, I forgot to mention he only directs films he writes, and he has always been an amazingly creative and funny writer. He had proven that years before he started writing and directing his films. He worked on Sid Caesar's Show of Shows as a writer with names like Carl Reiner, and Mel Brooks, and he was on their level. We finished the song then I went to get some craft services. I tell this story to show how a simple action can form a valuable bond. We connected over a mutual need to whistle. For you, it may be the way you both take your coffee. Maybe you notice the baseball cap of your team on her desk or the bong on his shelf. It could also be as simple as you both have kids. This is the way you connect while taking the scenic route.

Woody requested and booked me directly for his next film. You will hear about that amazingly golden experience later on.

Benefits of telling a great story: Paint the Picture

Tell me a story Daddy. I miss hearing that from my baby girl, my firstborn. Now my wife and I say, Sophie tells us stories over FaceTime. She is currently studying abroad in Valencia Spain and soaring!

People like a good story. We all have a story. Some are exciting, some are...not. Superheroes have an "Origin" story, why shouldn't you? When you share your stories, make sure to paint a full picture. Unless the bad chapters have a direct connection to what you are presenting, I suggest sharing only the interesting "cool" parts. The more "Oooh! Ahhh" moments help. These moments are in there.

Please, trust your Brains Operating Super System. IT can find these tidbits within your memory bank in a fraction of a millisecond. Share the experience impactfully, the emotions, and the feelings. The colors, the scent in the air to better sell your IT, your pitch should tell a story. When telling a story:

- Look to weed out any hesitation fillers ...fillers like: "You know" and "Like" or "So she said___, and he said___", more than once.
- Become the characters in your story...assign them different tones and voices.
- Help the audience or prospective client visualize being there themselves by creating the environment and trying to touch on as many senses that can make them feel.

Always remember people buy what makes them feel connected and comfortable.

Paint the visual picture for your audience. The more elaborate and colorful you can describe the environment; your story will take form.

The more detail you throw in, the better the listener or reader's imagination can build the world. It is also ok to fudge a bit. It's your story.

Example: Tell the prospect demand is high and competitors are also looking at it, or that you already have a deal in place, but do not enjoy working with the new contact. You would like to replace them with someone else in the same category. Do not tell lies but, add an extra cherry or funny element.

Let them use their imaginations to create the world you are sharing. If you tell them what it smells like or tastes like, it may help raise the stakes of the story.

Never Underestimate a Simple Compliment
Names are Important

Sometimes, my aging feeble mind still forgets a name I should remember. Especially when I just met this person 5 minutes ago. I learned a great way to cover that awkward moment. I am outing myself here. But, if I say "I'm sorry I forgot your name" or call them John when they are James, what does that tell the other person? What could they feel? You didn't care enough about them? Do you think you are too cool to remember them? You are a big poopiehead? Who knows what they take away from that awkward moment? That is why I say "Hey there, handsome or Lovely. It works on a goodbye too: Take care handsome. WOW, what a difference.

Instead of offending someone for not remembering who they are, you have made them feel good. What man doesn't like to be labeled as handsome, or a Woman told she is lovely. It is a cover-your-ass move, but it's also an earnest way to greet or exit.

Who you are, what you do, and why you should care are some of the things most people want you to know about them, especially after they've shared it with you. When you forget their name, some may feel discounted.

Have you ever met a person that didn't like a compliment? I have met many people who act as if they do not like getting complimented. They cannot accept a compliment without adding some comment demeaning themselves.

Talking with Two Thumbs

Other than Arthur Fonzerelli, people were not meant to communicate with just two thumbs. In today's age, amazing new technological wonders are being unveiled daily.

Why in the world have so many stopped communicating by voice? FaceTime even brings their face into view, but in my experience, people (my children and anyone younger than 30) hate it when I make a video call.

I do not like having to relay my communications; digitally sent through short soundbites and sentences. They are read in silence and replied to with a few words. Without a visual or a voice, our ability to observe the level of interest, and lack of enthusiasm, and get a clear sense of their happiness or frustration is severely hindered. Your true intention behind a text can be taken the wrong way by the other person participating in the exchange. A sender's message can lack a sense of emotion behind the words leaving you to wonder. Your ability to adjust based on their body language is taken away as texts can be misconstrued, and anger and upset can easily be created out of a false imagination, aka fantasy thinking. There is one benefit of texting, you can't see the pimple on the tip of my nose.

You may have heard the old term: "It's not what you say, it's the way you say it". The tone is the music. Words on paper can't speak as well as you can. Using your voice instead of text or even an email gives you more room whenever you can.

The real irony is much communication in 2024 is typically made using the high-tech version of the original device Mr. Bell initially created back in 1876. It's rarely used for that purpose anymore.

It is so much more than the telephone I grew up with.

If you were born after the turn of the century, and don't know who he is, he's the dude who invented the TelePhone, no iTelePhones existed yet. In a way, it was handheld but you were tethered to a plastic stationary odd shaped retro colored box on the wall or desk connected with a wire…click. First, you would hear a ringing noise, then the race was on. After a short battle with your sister, you arrive first to lift the…handle used for talking…and listening. It looked like a lopsided mini barbell. It had a ticking twisting dial with finger holes equally distributed for each number. Dialing one number could take 30 seconds. Mess up one number, a full minute! Ouch! Nooo! And get this, it was attached by a long squiggly expanding cord frequently used as a jump rope, or to do an impression of an orthodox Jewish guy very long payos. People would actually talk to other people and communicate using their real live voice, not thumbs if you can believe that. Someone located a distance away could just pick up a phone and say "Hi" using their words not basic short-form font. Using your voice more often, speaking up, and asking for what you want can be a game-changer for your life and career.

Improvisational abilities and focused awareness will equip you with the tools to establish authentic relationships with clients, bond with colleagues, and truly enjoy the time with partners or friends. It's about more than just business; it's about connections and evergreen relationships forged that go beyond the boardroom. Begin with Fun, and Finish with Profit.

As we journey together through this book, you'll begin to see these skills can have a direct impact on your bottom line. Improvisational Thinking can make your work not only more enjoyable, but also more profitable. It's not just about having fun; It's about developing lasting relationships, it's about closing deals, increasing revenue, and achieving unprecedented Unscripted $uccess.

Listen More - Talk Less

When you listen more and speak less, previously hidden Gems (or ideas) reveal themselves. You'll learn that silent but deadly, is not silent. Always have a pen and pad or your iPhone's Notes App, Voice Recorder App, or whatever you choose to use to write the GEM/Idea down so it doesn't vanish.

Remember, I am an ADHD poster child. A label I truly despise. I choose to refuse that label. I view it as hyper-awareness. Yes, there are some difficulties in having ADD or ADHD…Hyper-Awareness. One of my biggest hurdles in life is the ability to listen. I once heard the term "Take the cotton out of your ears, and put it in your mouth". My favorite Steven Covey saying would be in his 7 Habits. "Seek first to understand, then to be understood". That only happens by listening and downloading. It is also a great way to bond. Let them talk. Sometimes people just want to be heard. They want their thoughts or feelings validated. This goes for clients and prospects too. If they want to add an anecdote or story, listen and let them roll with it. Make sure to pay attention to what's being said, you may discover more than you know.

Valuable Lessons Come from Unexpected Places

It is amazing how much you can learn by simply asking questions and listening. Valuable lessons do come from unexpected places. Sometimes the larger lessons are already in your brain. Stored in random bits…then from out of nowhere, Bam!

An external trigger hits and your BOSS assembles the answer...these are the "Light bulb" or "A-Ha!" moments we all have. All of it is released from your brains data file cabinet, sense memory, and your pile of inner knowledge.

As you grow and improve, your needed skill set improves.

Through exploration, and remaining mindful, you will uncover what those skills will need to be. They will help you continue to find out how incredible you already are.

Here is an example of Self-Induced Stress from Fantasy Thinking. You are on your way to the airport. Traffic is heavier than you expected. The stress begins on I-95.

JOE AIRPLANE
(Building to extreme)
Why are you so late!? I am going to get
Stuck on a huge TSA security line!
Wow! You should've been here over 30 minutes ago!
I'll end up missing my friggin' plane! And great!
Now, I won't even have time to grab a bite!
My wife won't be able to pick me up!
I'll have to take the red eye! Ugh!
I'll miss my son's ballgame!
This is a catastrophe!

This is a perfect example of what I want to stick with you. This emotional state is brought in by worrying about a future scenario that never existed. None of those fears ever came to fruition. At some point in your life, you may have had a similar experience. Mad at yourself, mad at someone, or mad at the world, all because something happened that was not in the plan. Unexpected bullshit or self-created fear and anxiety build over what MIGHT now happen. You get yourself all worked up, only to see in the end, it didn't happen. You were early, you were able to grab a bite, make your plane, catch your son's ballgame, and get picked up by my beautiful wife. Yes, I am Joe Airplane. This exact whirlwind of upset happened to me flying back home from a business trip. I made myself nuts for no reason at all. Has something like this happened to you? So much wasted time and upsets. It all worked out perfectly. We feel silly for even being upset over what turned out to be your precious time, wasted on absolutely nothing but fantasy thinking.

"Mann Tracht, Un Gott Lacht" = Man Plans, G-d Laughs.

As an improvisational and stand-up comedian and as a salesman, I can only hope the audience comes with me and laughs. They MIGHT not?!? That's okay because I am confident, I can always adjust my material and reel them back in with the skills I have built. The key is trusting my gut, taking risks, and being completely present. I listen, look, and I am open to any offer or opportunity I see around me. If I'm thinking about something other than what is in front of me right now, I miss out on those offers and opportunities, and I typically lose.

Right Can be Wrong, and Wrong Can be Right

Sometimes some things can be both right and wrong at the same time. Here is a simple example of something you can be so sure of...but find out you are wrong. Technically. It's right, but it's wrong.

ME
Tell me if you can name this song.
(I whistle the melody to "Twinkle Twinkle Little Star".)

YOU
Twinkle Twinkle Little Star.

ME
No. It was ABCD. Let's do it again.
(I whistle the same song.)

YOU
Ok, That's Twinkle Twinkle.

ME

Nope. It's Baa Baa Black Sheep. One more time.
(Again, I whistle the same song.)

YOU

Ok that must be Twinkle Twinkle.

ME

Sure, that one's it!

They are all the same song. Only the words are different. Sometimes, like in the above example, we have the power to make someone wrong even though they can technically be right. Or vice versa. I suggest letting them be right. It always works better. Even if…you know ;o)

Remember the core tenet of Improvising is "Yes, and". Yes, and'ing works well in allowing others to be right. It helps move the process along (especially when it has no bearing on you or the outcome. Let it go).

Do not let yourself get caught up in the need to be right. If you think, or downright know you are right, what else do you truly need? When someone else disagrees with you, unless it's something like "No, I am sure I can swallow this razor blade. I'll be fine." Let them win. By letting them win, you win. I know that is high-level cheesy, but true nonetheless. By releasing your desire to have to be right, you allow yourself and the other person to move on to the next thing you can agree on.

I started a new business called Comedyation. Comedy + Mediation = Comedyation.com. We take conflict and turn it into comedy. You would be surprised how many people live with conflict for the simple reason of having to be right. The word right can be confusing as it has so many meanings and spellings.

Example: I don't have to be Right when I Write this sentence about Orville Wright landing Right in the field and sitting on the Right side of the tent to celebrate their nephew completing his sacred Rite of marriage…to Susan Ryght. It was a Riot!

Should we care about what people say?

Yes and no. Yes, reviews and opinions can affect your success, but only if you really allow them to. You can become paralyzed in upset from one bad review.

For example, I had the exciting experience of sharing a small theater with a group of around 250 people over a weekend. I did a few workshops, gave a fun interactive lecture, and emceed the final Global event. I happily finished to a standing ovation. I felt fantastic. Afterward, I overheard someone dissing my entire program. They didn't like anything about it and couldn't understand how and why it was so well received. That one person's thoughts and words destroyed my fantastic feeling. I allowed their thinking to alter my thinking. I discounted the other 249 people and focused only on the one. I have seen this with comedians too. One of the best "A-List" Comics I've ever known was rolling along. I'd say he is a comedian's comedian. Perfect at this craftiness, I'd venture to say he is probably on most comedian's top 10 list. He was killing it. Until he noticed one person in the audience with their arms crossed, not smiling or laughing at the comic's strongest material. This comic was a true master of the craft, he didn't like knowing he couldn't please everyone so he would now make the conscious choice to focus on this one person, and in doing so, he lost the rest of the room. Do not fret, as I said, this guy is a national headliner and before he was done, he had won the room back and as always, he crushed it.

Both of the above experiences (my 1 out of 250 or his one

audience member) helped to teach me a great lesson. A simple lesson summed up by the old saying "You can't please everyone". Someone may not like what you do for silly reasons only known to them. Trust in your content, deliver it to the best of your ability and disregard the haters. These are people who do not like rainbows, babies, or puppies.

I mean come on, who doesn't like...puppies? Therefore, why should you care about their opinions?

Petey The Dog

Speaking of puppies, back in 1986, I had great luck getting a job working at Shea Stadium for the TV station with the local broadcast coverage. It was some of the best times of my life. One perk of the job was getting to know the lady who handles the tickets for the team. We had access to the best tickets. For example, we liked sitting with the player's wives.

One day, my brother Jamie, introduced me to a fun bartender from his neighborhood named Bobby. We would go have a couple of drinks and talk with Bobby about the Mets. Yes, he is also afflicted with the same tragic disorder...being a Mets fan. He is also the most impressive tailgate chef I've ever met to this day. We're talking lobster, filet mignon, shrimp scampi, and more. Not the kind of food you would expect to be served in a parking lot. Bobby would take all day long preparing for the day's pre-game tailgate menu.

One weekend I offered to pick him up on our way to the stadium. When we walked in the first thing that happened was an extremely excited large Pitbull/Black lab mix came running up, and stuck his nose in my crotch. Making his presence known.

The house smelled amazing as he was knee-deep in sautéing

mushrooms with shallots, to be stuffed inside some kind of fancy meat. While he was cooking, he asked us if we would be willing to take Petey for a walk. We accepted the mission. As we were walking out of the door, Bobby said it shouldn't take too long just make a right, a right, a right, and a right back in the building. I noticed Bobby chuckling.

Petey was a sweet young dog. He was very strong and was clearly on a mission. You can truly feel the strength of this dog by the pressure of his pulling me easily from standing to having to run.

We get dragged around the first corner. The tug of war continued until we got closer to the next corner. As we approached the corner to make our second right turn, Petey stopped pulling. We had slack on the leash. He slowly walks up to the corner barks loudly twice and freezes. Jaime and I look at each other. Huh? Just then from across the street, we hear a large dog barking. Not the kind of bark that you would want to approach. Within seconds a very large German Shepherd is behind a tall, sturdy fence surrounding the entire property. The moment Petey saw that the dog was behind the fence and not free. This tugging beast turned into a prancer. Like a horse doing dressage or a pretty pampered poodle.

He didn't pull us, but he was very clear. He wanted to go across the street to the fence. We didn't think that was a good idea, but he did not care what we thought, he was going to say hello to the big vicious, growling dog.

As we approached the fence, that dog was losing his shit. If he could've gotten out of that fence, I believe he might've eaten me whole, but he was behind the fence locked away.

Petey calmly strolled up to the patch of grass that was on our side of the fence. He walked up to the other dog calmly staring at its foaming face. Showing absolute disregard for the other dogs' clear communication of, "I would kick your ass if only I could get out of here!" Petey did not care, as he trotted around in a circle. The shepherd is blowing his top at this point knowing what is about to happen. After a few circles, Petey looks at the dog, turns, and faces the complete opposite direction showing his backside to the dog. He then commenced his mission. Before we can grab this lovely gift, Petey makes it clear, it's for the Shepherd. He gives us a look almost as if he is saying: "Hey, watch this" and starts ripping up the grass and the dirt with all four paws, throwing the nasty mélange of grass, dirt, and poop! We watched the debris fly violently into the sharply fanged face of what must be Petey's biggest nemesis.

As soon as Petey threw his last crap-collection, he let loose with one of the most vicious attacks barks I have ever witnessed. The anger, the cursing (Yes, I speak dog and know all the curse words) His screaming back at the other dog seemed to work. The other dog shut up. After a few moments, Petey also stops silent. He shoots us a look. Ha! He turns and starts calmly prancing away. We followed him laughing all the way home.

When we arrived, the first thing Bobby said was "Was the shepherd out?" We said yup. That was unbelievable. Bobby informed us that this happens every time that dog is outside. He also tells us why his dog has such animosity towards the German Shepherd. When he first got Petey, he had been out for a walk, when that dog had gotten loose and came out of nowhere, and bit Petey before they could hold him back.

Petey needed the fence between them for him to be comfortable. Even though he is a different species, Jamie and I understood his communication with us and his bully. Petey just needed to know he was safe to be himself. It was another perfect example of inter-species communication. Jaime and I had no questions about what was being communicated. It also shows how trauma in our youth can affect us for years to come.

If you want, you can take a moment to think about one traumatic event that still exists and still bothers your conscious thoughts when it pops up. Acknowledge that this trauma did happen. You experienced it, and it is now gone! History! Ancient Times! Other than being cautious the next time, that's not a thought to spend a moment on anymore. If the thought is not helping you, change the thought.

Smiles are Contagious: Let Your Funny Out

Laughing together helps create strong bonds. Especially when another person feels comfortable enough to say what they are thinking, or feeling without judgment. It feels good to know someone else finds the same things you find funny.

When you make someone or even yourself laugh, good energy surrounds the moment. You need to know your audience but do not be afraid to be silly. Fun and funny always make things better, ease tension, and creates smiles.

Spreading Smiles

Both a true smile and an authentic laugh can be contagious. Growing up in a family with a naturally funny father was great. He taught us the concept of "Make them smile, then make them laugh". It wasn't as if he sat us down and explained the theory. We just saw him do it with ease. He easily won over any waiter with an attitude, a car salesman trying to gouge him, and even a policeman trying to give him a speeding ticket. This showed me that having this ability and a strong sense of humor was a valuable asset. An asset I would eventually learn to not only master but happily share what I've learned by teaching these methods and funny formulas. From a silly voice or face, to joke formulas when delivered correctly, these can induce that smile.

When I began my mid-life years, I wanted a Corvette, but I didn't fit in one. But it was ok because I was beyond delighted to book the role of a lifetime. I was about to turn 40 years old. Up until then, I had not had the opportunity or experience of acting in a scripted play, or musical at any time in my life. My world was all improvisation, sketch, and stand-up comedy. I turned 40 the week of my Broadway debut. I was performing in a scripted play written by the great Neil Simon. I have been blessed to perform on Broadway twice more. I was now creating a sea of smiles nightly. Many 1,000's of faces smiling every week!

"I Went from Never to Nirvana."
- Me

Like a sneeze, or a hiccup, a true smile is involuntary. It is the same for an authentic laugh. In most cases, we only laugh when something or someone instantly stimulates our senses to react positively. No one has ever said, "I didn't have fun while I was laughing". Walls are torn down when you can get someone to laugh! It says to another person, okay, we're cool. Their defenses are let down and a smile follows and is invariably accompanied by a laugh as, for a split second, you've touched their soul. If only for a moment, Status, Ego, and need for Power are instantly removed. This is how kings and citizens' bond. The court jester was always nearby to help the king get into a good mood...or he was an easy kill! Off with his head! Why would a chicken cross the road anyway!?

JOHN: Knock Knock...

BOB: Who's there?

JOHN: Simon. The interrupting cow.

BOB: Simon the interrupt...

JOHN: (Interrupting) Moo.

A simple joke set up in a simple format. A format every preschooler probably knows. But regardless, it's a silly joke that usually works on anyone at any age.

One-liners are easy to remember. People like a good Pun.

- I had a Taser once. It was stunning.
- I used to hate facial hair, but then it grew on me.
- I don't trust trees. They're shady.

The 7th Sense - A Sense of Humor

There are moments when the funny just pops out at me. I do believe it is an inherited trait. Incorporating funny formulas into what you are sharing can raise interest. You can take a sad, bad, or unfortunate situation and find a way to slide in a bit of humor. There was a time when I was staring at the reality of virtually $0.00 in the bank, $0.00 in savings, less than $0 net worth. I felt like a great big Zero. Looking back on those grim days, I can still find the funny in it. I had little money, who knew moose knuckle could be so delicious? I had to take a side job as a Panda in the zoo, the costume sucked, but the free food was excellent.

Once you see or sense you may have a setup in your path, jump on that shit! For example, earlier I wrote about being fortunate to have money growing up. Did I mention in my video games, real people die? Now is that true? No, but it fits the setup. After a while, you will start finding opportunities to capitalize on this kind of formula.

All you need is a simple setup. What is a setup? The "I Was a

Rich Kid" bit started with a simple setup line. The format is similar to that old game show, Match Game. All I needed was the foundation line. I was so rich___. Or, we had so much money___. I then locked and loaded on punchlines. Here area few worthy rejects.

A. My parrot spoke three languages.
B. My treehouse was timeshared.
C. I never touched my own penis until I was 18. I had an official shaker in the bathroom.

Now can you think of three more?

With a Joke or Humorous lines like these, or whatever you come up with using the same formula for D... E... & F, your client or audience will laugh…or chuckle…or worst case, they just simply smile.

Making smiles is what it is all about. Either way, you will still raise the humor level while still hitting your point. In email format, sometimes clever is just as good as funny.

What's so Funny?

What is funny? Is humor a trait that can be passed down, or transferable? Is it universal? Most comedians will say, "You are either funny or you are not." As a veteran of the funny, I can agree…to a point. So, how can you teach someone to be funny?

You could find and learn how to tell jokes, mine a tickle of humor from almost anything, and create your smile-inducing moments. Would you like to be better at sharing your sense of humor? I think so.

Here are some tips, techniques, and formulas that will assist you and your team in raising your level of humor. Even if your joke dies, know that humor can be subjective. I feel if it is funny, it's funny. You cannot please them all. You can however be the best prepared.

Know your Audience - This is extremely important. If you are speaking to a room of church members, you may speak differently than if you were speaking at the Arm-Wrestling Association. Find as much background information on who will be there. It is helpful.

Jokes - Tell a Joke - Learn a few great jokes. Clean Jokes and perhaps a few dirty jokes. Take your time to master those jokes. Each time you tell it you can adjust a bit until you find your delivery. As joke books go, I believe the New York City Cab Drivers Joke Book series by Jim Pietsch is the best collection of jokes I've ever seen assembled. Jokes from all types, and all age levels, from clean jokes to blue or dirty jokes.

Set-up → Punchline - Jokes don't always just appear to a comedian. There is work that must be done to get to the gold. As I explained in "The 7th Sense - A Sense of Humor", once you find the setup line, lock and load to find your best punchline

Example: I was so rich.

Always Open Strong - Just like standing on the comedy stage, any presentation or discussion that you hope to get others to buy in on or agree to your request, it is always important to open strong. I suggest beginning on a topic that has nothing to do with the business at hand. Maybe mention something topical or personal. Take the scenic route by entertaining their senses. I used to open with a harmonica. And close with a singing bit. A closer is helpful too.

The Rule of Three - Three is the magic number in comedy. Some call it the triple and it is a foundational theory of comedy and writing. You may not notice it, but you've seen it everywhere. A Beginning, a Middle, and an End. Act I, Act II Act III. A standard triple.

A Priest, A Rabbi, and A Duck Walk into a bar…

You can make two statements and after the third comes the rimshot. Three also sets up a pattern. It also lets you heighten the stakes.

Example: Welcome to Munchy's. We serve Burgers, Pizza, and Pot.

Heightening - When you can raise the stakes, it helps move things along. Another great improviser, Will Hines, defines heightening as "hitting a comedic idea several times in a way that gets more absurd as you go." Will is the author of the book, "How to Be the Greatest Improviser on Earth". It is fantastic.

Example: A great example of heightening was performed by my improv mentor Pat "the Vampire" Battistini. (Ask me about how he once ate a tree to win a car.) Pat was doing a scene where he had to translate a toothpick to another player. Like charades, you could not use any English. It is similar to mime, but we call this object work. Creating something as a needed prop out of thin air and making it visually believable. Sound effects and gibberish were also allowed. Showing someone a toothpick would typically be an easy task. Hold a small imaginary pointy thing and pick at your teeth. Nope, not Pat. He started as a manly lumberjack character. He then chopped down a large tree, Chainsawed a large branch, he then completed whittling it down to a toothpick, and simply picked his teeth. Oh! Holy Christmas! It's a toothpick! Ha, that was so cool.

Exchange / Reversal - When you switch something out that doesn't necessarily fit, it can lead to a laugh. Exchanging one thing for another non-traditional thing is one of the easier mechanisms that lift the humor level.

Examples: Having Ozzy Osbourne delivering a Sermon in Church, or Seeing a Cat and a Mouse in a relationship, or watching a dog walking a human.

Over-Emphasizing - When you over-emphasize things on purpose for the sake of humor and not drama, it can be a helpful tool.

Example: I was so fat when I jumped up in the air...I got stuck!

Opposites - Yin and Yang, Black and White, Men and Women. Each has its counterpart. You can take two things that are on the opposite sides of the scale and bounce them off each other. Switching up the expectations of your audience.

Good - Bad, Wealthy - Poor, Slow - Fast, Sharer - Selfish, Happy - Unhappy, Wild - Calm, Best - Worst, Quiet - Loud, Hard - Soft, Hate - Love, Gender - Gender, etc... Beauty and the Beast, Detective and Criminal, Dog and Cat...Different, although not necessarily contrary are possible.

Example: Who knew Quasimodo was dating Kim Kardashian? This leads me to…

Exaggerated Comparisons - Comparing one thing with another somewhat, off-base thing can work in many spots.

Example: I would rather have Johnny Knoxville and his friends babysit my child. I'm not letting that nurse near my kids. Scares me like, having a razorback gorilla scheduled as my masseuse. Them getting married is like a swan marrying a frog. (add a reversal) I wonder if he kisses her will she turn into a princess?

Author and Humorist Terry Pratchett wrote: "The difference

between erotic and pornographic: it's like using a feather instead of the whole chicken."

Physical Comedy - Names like Buster Keaton, Dick Van Dyke, Jim Carrey, John Ritter, Chevy Chase, and the great Bill Irwin were known for their ability to manipulate their bodies in odd, funny ways. Today it's Jackass, Punked, and…Martha Stewart.

Sometimes to their detriment they'd perform in ways that would break others. Pratfalls, Pranks, and even Limbs ripped off and blood gushing out with zero reaction by the limbless (See Monty Python and the Holy Grail). Bodies moving in shocking, odd, silly, scary ways will always get a reaction. We cannot forget the master format for physical comedy, Cartoons.

Ever since the introduction of animation, the limits were lifted. You could Squish, Stretch, Smash, Anvils falling on heads…Splatt, getting up and walking away. Incorporate gestures, facial expressions, or physical actions to enhance your jokes. Visual movement and other physical elements can complement verbal humor and engage a broader range of audience members…and clients.

Example: Walking unsuspectedly and stepping onto a rake. It pops up and hits you in the face. Slipping on a banana peel is extreme, but they're classic bits.

Write - When you have a pitch or need to prepare yourself to dazzle, I suggest taking the time to research the subjects or targets for the day. If you can get some friendly spies in the company to give you background info, you can sit and write out some ideas, find some setups, and write a bunch of punchlines you may never use. One will do. Keep no more than the top 3.

Self-Deprecation / Making Fun of Yourself - Making light-hearted jokes about your own experiences, flaws, or mishaps helps your audience relate to you. A silly play on empathy or pity can be great for bonding with each other. "Gina broke up with you too?" Just keep it good-natured to endear yourself to your audience.

Example: "I asked my mirror if I'm the fairest of them all. It laughed. We're getting a new mirror."

Timing - Practice the delivery of your lines, bits, or jokes to ensure they land at the right moment. Pausing can be just as crucial as the punchline. Use them strategically for emphasis. Don't worry so much about silence. That means they are listening.

Example: Years ago, a comedian named Henny Youngman was working at an event and brought his wife. Before he went on stage, he asked a stagehand "Take my wife, please". The stagehand thought it was a joke and laughed. Henny threw it into his act. At first, there was no reaction. He had added a few words…Excuse me, sir, can you please take my wife…nope. Sir, can you please take my wife…nope. After several variations, he ended up back to the simple four words. "Take my wife, please". This timing worked best.

When you are selling, take that beat. Let whatever you are putting out there sink in for a moment, then hit the line. Joke or not, pacing…and…timing can make…a…big difference.

Surprise/Twist - You can build anticipation and then flip expectations with an unexpected turn. Misdirection can keep your audience guessing until the punchline. Magicians often use this comedic technique to enhance and add icing to their prestidigitation.

Example: When I was much heavier, I had a joke that worked

well. I'd say: "I weighed 185 lbs. when I met my first wife… (I'd then rub my belly and start picking my teeth…wait that beat…Then say) She mysteriously disappeared". If I didn't time it well it would bomb. What was funny, is for some in the audience, the timing of the laugh was delayed. About a minute after the joke, the surprise twist hits them...Huh? Oh my gosh, He ate her?!?! Haha, that is funny"...Keep up with the jokes people.

Exaggeration - Identify relatable situations and then exaggerate the details to the point of absurdity. You can use hyperbole to emphasize and magnify the funny in everyday events.

Example: As the guys all sit around talking about their manhood, bragging… I would say: "Yeah, well I am hung like a tic tac" ...I'd get a laugh…(beat)...No, actually…(Beat)...I am hung like a two-year-old…...(longer beat)……The entire child". Without that longer second beat, it is not as effective.

Wordplay/Puns/Limericks - You can play with language, and gibberish, exploiting multiple meanings or sounds of words. Remember, know your audience. Age and language comprehension to ensure they catch the wordplay.

- Example: Pun - I used to be a baker because I kneaded dough.
- Example: Limerick - There once was a lady from Spain, she would always get caught in the rain, she wore a white shirt, and pulled off her wet skirt, while the men all just stared at her…Brain

The format is a simple AABBA pattern. A's Rhyme with A's. B's rhymes with B's.

Observational Comedy - Pay attention to what's going on around you. Offers and opportunities abound. You see something that is silly and you shine light on it in a clever way. It doesn't always have to be a joke. People-watching is always a great space. Just wait and witness bizarre behaviors and find the quirks you may never have noticed.

You can often find humor in shared experiences. Highlight the absurdities of everyday life that often go unnoticed.

Example: "We'd let our parakeet out of his cage, he'd fly around the room, BANG! He'd fly right into the mirror and bang his little head! I'd always think, even if he thinks the mirror is another room, why doesn't he at least try to avoid hitting the other parakeet?"

- Jerry Seinfeld

Many of these observations are mutually recognized experiences. Some of which have never been spoken, or we all know, but do not speak of it.

Incongruity - Combine unrelated topics, items, and thoughts in a way that creates an amusing contrast. Think about unexpected pairings that provoke laughter due to their surprising connection.

Example: "I tried to make a sandwich with the ingredients I had on hand: peanut butter, strawberry jam, and lox. Surprisingly, not a hit." (lox aka smoked salmon).

Satire - Using irony and sarcasm can highlight the wacky, the silly, the flaws or absurdities in our own lives and society. Shifting, cultural norms or situations. Be aware of your audience's sensibilities to avoid crossing sensitive boundaries.

Example: "I read a book on anti-gravity. It's impossible to put down."

Callbacks - Sometimes referring back to something from an earlier line, joke or shared experience can elicit a chuckle or more. It's called a callback. It makes the audience feel like they are "in on it'. They're getting the second joke because you hit them with the premise earlier. It works well, it becomes something they shared with you. A callback works when an earlier joke or bit hits, it creates a sense of cohesion in your comedic performance and strengthens the connection with your audience. Callbacks are great but do not overdo them. Remember the Rule of Three.

Telling Stories - When telling stories, keep your audience engaged by painting that picture as richly as possible. Tickle their senses. What was the environment like, colors, how it smelled or felt like, who was there? Give them every nook and cranny so they can truly immerse their minds in your words.

Improvised Opportunities - Keep the good improvs. When something spontaneous happens, and it gets a nice laugh, pocket it. It's now material and a new card in your pocket to pull out if the opportunity arises again.

Becoming the Characters - When telling a story that has a few characters, a simple adjustment in your voice to differentiate each character will raise the smile level. I find audiences always find character voices amusing.

Impressions - Can you do an impression of someone or mimic something universally heard? If so, it is an effective skill. Even if they aren't celebrity impressions. You can create your own impressions. Here is my grandma at a strip club, "Oh boy, that's wondaful. Oooh". This is my mother-in-law telling dirty limericks. You can have your cast of voices. Your voice is higher or lower or raspy, maybe a lisp. Speakingof the listhp. I use it in silly characters that have different lisps. I do three different styles of lispy voices.

Firetruck moment: My daughter and middle son both had lisps. This was not desired with the name Sietz - S and Z. Oy! I broke it with a simple cure. Hey, close your teeth when an "s" sound comes up. It worked both times. Now they make the bessst S's. Ah Ha! Sietz, not Thietzz (BTW its Sights, not Seats). I love doing impressions. For me, it started with Kermit the Frog, we are currently on voicemail messages as Peter Griffin. Just know that a bad impression can be detrimental.

Accents - Like impressions, accents have always come easy to me. Perhaps it's kind of a savant gift of my neurodiverse brain. I am always amazed at how much enjoyment others get out of a silly accent or voice. They can't believe I can switch so easily. Using an accent can win. I suggest only doing an accent other people (not just yourself) agree sounds authentic. If not, don't do it. Like bad impressions, a bad accent can be detrimental.

True Experiences vs. Fictitious Experiences - Humor often comes from the truth being revealed. When telling your own authentic stories you can refer to memory. Not all stories have to be completely real. Fantastic tales of the wild, the whimsy, and the wicked are always accepted…as long as they don't suck.

A little fudge or a complete fabrication is not out of the question if it's a good one. You are telling a story. It is not a news report.

Family Members / Siblings / Spouses / Children / Only Children & Pets - are all fountains of fun. You know them well and they may even know you better than you know yourself. In most cases, they are your first and most honest audience. Tap into that. You will find family gems (not family jewels). You can mine real honest gold.

I have used these comedy techniques and formulas for almost a half-century. These skills have allowed me to do what I love every day. Funny has given me opportunities to sell, perform, and act on some of the top television shows, and films, write for other comedians, and ad agencies, and perform at clubs and theaters internationally.

Experiment with these techniques and formulas, and remember that humor is subjective, so being keyed into your audience's reactions is essential. The more opportunities you get to present your presentation, jokes, or ideas, the better you get. Each time you tighten it up, adjust and refine your approach based on what is or is not working for your audience.

Roasting...Yourself

Roasting someone or engaging in a little self-deprecation can be funny for several reasons. A lot of the funny relies on the unexpected or placing stuff where it doesn't belong. Highlight contrasting outrageous alternatives to true situations. In the comedy world, roasting is part of the culture. Being asked to be roasted is an honor. Getting to participate as a guest on the dais, and doing the roasting is also an honor. A roast often involves saying something unexpected or contrary to what one might typically expect in a social situation. Self-deprecation involves humorously undermining one's self-image. These unexpected twists can provoke laughter. For example, nobody is off limits. If you attend, you are fair game. No topic is off the table. Being the Roastee can be a helpful eye-opening experience. This particular comedy helps us learn to laugh at ourselves and serve up some greater material for future self-deprecation.

For Example...again:

"I was so fat when I jumped up in the air, I'd get stuck".

Bonding, in mutual destruction. Roasting is often done in a sarcastically friendly way, playful manner among friends, or a group setting. It can strengthen relationships (or destroy them). Picking on each other is a form of bonding. A zing or a comeback demonstrates a level of comfort and trust within the group. When someone is willing to engage in self-deprecation or allow others to roast them, it can create a sense of camaraderie. Roasting each other and ourselves can release tension. It allows us to speak on private, sensitive topics and any truly authentic relationships you have within your lifelong network. As a comedic performer, it is paramount for your audience to like you or you are doomed.

Your attitude or personal flaws indirectly and in a funny lighthearted way. By laughing at ourselves or each other, we can deal with potentially uncomfortable or awkward situations more easily. Self-deprecating humor gives us a way to make a connection in a relatable way. When people hear someone joking about something they do it themselves. In sharing their flaws or insecurities, it can make them feel like they're not alone in their imperfections. This relatability can generate laughter and a sense of connection with like-minded folks.

Self-deprecation can show others you, like anyone else, have your vulnerabilities. I find when people share vulnerabilities, it can make them more endearing or relatable. It's like saying, "I'm human, too," and this can be quite charming and funny. Like a fart. In many cultures, this friendly verbal self-abuse (that is an oxymoron) is viewed by others as a sign of humility and openness. People who take themselves too seriously are not as fun as those who can handle the ribbing and insensitive words. Humor that shows humility can be appreciated. Just remember, roasting and self-deprecation should be done in good taste and with consideration for the feelings of others. What's funny to one person might be hurtful to another. So, know your audience so you can measure the social reaction and the individuals involved to ensure that such humor is well-received. Brad Bitterly and Alison Wood Brooks from the Harvard Business Review Said:

"Can one joke make a meaningful difference in how people are viewed by others? In our study, the answer was unequivocally Yes."

Jokes at Another's Expense

Is it Funny or Mean? Sarcasm or just Rude? Humor can be used as a tactical Weapon. There is a fine line between bullying and a little pecking order. This is an important business experience between kids…and adults. The same thing happens in the office at home and between friends. Men will razz their friends. Yes, it would be nice for all to get along all the time. That is not reality, all of us experience conflict at some point in life (If and when you do, go to comedyation.com). Some of these experiences are important as we learn from them and bank what we learn for another day. If you are not a professional, remember this…Jokes go along well with kindness. Unless you are at a Friars Roast or the comics table roasting the other comics, or an insult comic dog…for me to poop on.

Beyond a roast, a joke is not a joke if it is at the expense of another person. At some point in life, we may be treated like an outcast. It is the same feeling that comes up when a kid…let's say, Timmy. Timmy sees an Instagram post with all of his friends. They're all swimming, laughing and having a blast. Timmy didn't know about it, didn't get invited, and now he feels yucky. He finds out the reason was that KICK ME sign he taped on Lucy Conklin's back in the high school hallway. He didn't even think about that. Someone else getting kicked in the ass all morning had zero effect on Timmy. Now on he gets a taste of the other end.

"The human race has only one really effective weapon and that is laughter."
- Mark Twain

Humor is subjective, being unkind is not. I must stress again, that if you are thinking about being funny with words or actions, please take a moment to consider your audience, and ask yourself, could it harm another person? If so, don't. You cannot and should not attempt to build happiness on someone else's pain.

Love: Life's Most Valuable Commodity

I believe Love is a premium high-test fuel for a human being. Without it, we break down".

Growing up, we all establish fairly quickly that money can get us stuff. It's only natural to want new stuff, different stuff, just a little more once in a while.

You can gain vast wealth based on your hard work, skill, luck, or maybe an inheritance from your rich uncle Goopy. However, you get your money, as long as you have enough to make sure you can afford somewhere to sleep safely, food, transportation, and the ability to communicate with others, smartphone and internet, of course…all is good.

Many people do not have this freedom or sense of security. It is a bit odd that the human race finds it OK for one person to have more than an entire country. How about someone who will spend $100 million on a boat, excuse me…Yacht. While just one % of that could feed a small village for a year or more. Whatever floats your yacht…I mean boat.

I do not begrudge anyone that has earned it and wants to spend it. For me, it's not about the dollar, it's more about the love, friendship, comfort, safety, and support when I need it. Sounds a little corny right? Yes, it does. But, in my experience, those who are not in a happy place, typically do not have love and support. Some do and are just a downer. I believe some criminals risk their lives and their freedom because no one's here to give them love and support. It's sad when I see parents speaking to their children with such anger when they've done something silly like spill their water, drop their ice cream cone, or whack dad in the nuts with his toy golf club.

If you think about it, most of your happy moments have come

when you're surrounded by love. Sometimes you could be all alone in your room, and… Well, that's a different kind of loving yourself.

I used to get way caught up in wanting to be rich and famous and have whatever I wanted, and I wanted everything and anything I could collect. Cool things and money for more awesome things. It's nice to have stuff and it's nice to have money, but I'm sure you've heard it before, even with money and stuff many people are not happy. Like The Beatles said. "Money can't buy you Love".

I was caught up in my head, thinking negatively about most issues. My glass was always half empty. I did not spend enough time doing more things with the people I love and care about me. You would be surprised how a simple phone call just to say "Hey, I was just thinking about you. How are you doing? What's shaking'?" will brighten up that person's day, show up with an extra coffee, make plans to do something…Unless you owe them money.

Stop! Right now, think about someone you haven't spoken to in a while that you miss. You know the kind of person I'm talking about. Someone you have not connected with for a long time, but the moment you're together, it's as if no time has passed.

If there's more than one, list them. Now commit to at least calling one of those people on the list. If you're feeling up to it, tell them to grab their calendar and make plans while you have them on the phone. They were just sitting there watching the ducks, ducks and more ducks channel, and bam, you called and brightened their day. You will be happily surprised with every call to those people in your life who would LOVE to hear from YOU!

Every time I see someone sleeping on the street, in traffic holding a sign for money, having to beg for food. I want to shower them with love…and an actual shower. Whew! I'm guessing Love was something lacking in their life at that moment. Love is a major high-test fuel for a human being. Money can buy you stuff, but you could have all the money in the world and many false claims of love and still be miserable. I believe all people just want to feel loved, accepted, and worthy.

Finances and other key issues like drug use, mental illness and crime come from a sense of longing to be a part of something and may not be picked or not included at all. These are all major factors that contributed to their situation.

Chapter 6
Improvisational Thinking in Business

* * *

The Journey Ahead

With the foundation laid and the principles of Improvisational Thinking at your disposal, we will look ahead to the exciting possibilities that await you. Your journey in business, sales, and life in general is just beginning the process of improving your mind's ability to react to the unexpected. Armed with these newfound skills, you'll be ready to face the challenges that come your way.

I find acronyms can be clever, silly, and helpful in helping me remember and get things I want done, done. Here are a few clever, silly and stupid acronyms I've thought of:

TIMED = Things I Must Effectively Do

LIFE = Living Inside Feeling Excellent

MUST = Manage Understanding Self Trust

GULP = Get Up Live Purpose

MONEY = Many Obstacles Never Ending Yearning

TAKER = The Act of Keeping Everything Received

ACRONYM = Another Creative Rouse Overtly Nullifying Young Minds

OR … A Crazy Read of Nonsense You Master

OR … Another Crappy Reworking Of my New York Mets

I do have a couple of favorites I made up to help me stay focused, on track, and on time. The first one I made up and used myself is what I like to call…" Getting PACKED up for the day".

Getting PACKED up for the Day

Pack a bag, we are going on a trip. But first, we must get P.A.C.K.E.D. up. I am always PACKED. This way, I am always ready to go. I am always on call for the unexpected. I am prepared because:

I am…**P**resent and **P**urposeful

I take…**A**ccountable **A**ction

I stay…**C**onsciously **C**ommitted

And I am…**K**ind to the **K**ing* (Myself)

So, I can…**E**volve **E**very day

And **D**iscover and **D**o **D**aily

(I know, * What if you're not a King? What if you are a **L**ikeably **G**allant **B**eautiful **T**rue **Q**ueen? I thought of making it…um…**K**ween. A clever way to cover the Q in Queen. Sorry, The Q would squash my wordplay. But that's not why I chose not to go there. I couldn't. No disrespect, it's just seeing those 3 Ks bolded in a row, has a yucky flavor to it, so please understand why I left it at King and know I allow anyone of valor and worthiness to ascend to King in my universe.

Unlike the K, I do not have any issues with three D's. I love it when there are two of them, so why would I have an issue with triple D's?

Present - Accountable - Conscious - Kind - Evolve - Daily

Present and Purposeful

Staying Present and taking purposeful action returns the best value of your time. Let's say you are at work, you have a list of prospects to call but today, you are having a hard time. You're in a bad mood, sad, anxious, envious, or (fill in your own blank).

One simple step that has helped me stay mindful for years now. I guess it's a form of meditation, power nap, or self- hypnosis maybe? Find a space where you can be alone, will not get interrupted, and get comfy. Close your eyes, deep breathing in through your nose. When you've had enough, prepare for a kiss and start to slowly release the air by imagining you are blowing out of a tiny coffee straw. Repeat this until you can barely tell where you are and what you are resting on. You kind of melt into it. When you get there, tell yourself (Out loud or in your head), I will live in the present. Keep your focus on what is before you and shut the door on any negative thoughts. Get out of your head. Do not allow your thoughts of the past, or of the future to enter for now. This process helps me complete those things I want to do. I keep myself on point by doing what I am meant to be doing. If I am exhausted, it helps a lot. I quickly give myself a quick reboot. I take those 5 minutes to get myself re-energized and re-centered by bringing my mind back to the NOW. If you have more time? That power nap of 20 minutes also does wonders. When we are children, we take naps. When we are elderly, we take naps. It won't kill you (or anyone else) to take a few moments to yourself to shut down and reboot your BOSS. You'll deliver a better you.

Accountable Action

Self-Accountability was and still is a huge must for my sanity and growth. It was missing from my vocabulary for a long time. Taking action heals me, and it will heal you. Getting real helps you to Master your Mojo.

The Action gets things started. Accountability gets it done.

Inaction and wasted time begin to rot your soul and putrefy your goals. Do not keep wondering...If only. Take action. Make IT happen.

Action is key to getting what you want and to find out what you are made of. Make this moment the day you became a better person to yourself, not having to sell bullshit excuses ever again. Selling it becomes natural. You become a self-starting selling machine because you're not just selling it, you're connecting and making project partners. By taking responsibility for your words, actions, and behaviors and owning the bullshit, you can leave the excuses behind you.

Sure, an Accountability Coach is great. Can you afford one? Do you need one? They won't take the fork or plate away or get you to move your body to sweat. You must do it on your own, or stop yourself from lighting up that Marlboro...light. Or, wearing that horrible outfit you wore at that thing at that place. YOU are stronger than you know. Take action. Walk the walk.

Consciously Committed

When you are on your game, you are focused, you are not just talking, you are taking action. It is happening, and it's the best way to keep up the momentum long-term. You must make a decision and commit. Someone once gave me a great definition of a True Decision. A true decision is like crossing the bridge and then immediately blowing it up behind you so you have no way back. Mentally decide to commit to yourself. You will see everything fall into place. Go ahead and congratulate yourself.

The little wins build on the last. When trying to lose weight, just driving by Louie's Ice Cream Shop and not stopping was a win for me. More often than not, when I ask, I receive. When I'm in the supermarket after I've lost a bunch of weight I stand on my tippy toes, reaching for something on a high shelf and my jeans fall to my ankles. Yes, I did embarrass myself, but to me, it is still a win!

Kind to the King

Self-doubt always crept in and then I would commence beating myself up. Too many times I would lose my shit over silly unimportant things like making a mistake filling out a form in ink, missing a right turn, and now having to drive 1.7 miles out of my way to make a U-turn or not getting to that last slice in time used to kick my ass. For me to keep standing up, something I need to do is let myself off the hook.

Evolve Every Day:

Today builds on yesterday. Find your strength, and see the growth. Wake up and accomplish something. Anything. Make your bed, email a friend or your mother, make the kids breakfast.

Do more good deeds. They will not hurt, and you will feel good.

Discover & Do it Daily:

Explore your world to find new stuff to learn about. Explore more.

Pay attention to your surroundings and not your inner thoughts. You will discover daily. Find one thing each day that will help you learn something new.

Self-Perspective

"Self-approval and self-acceptance in the now are the main keys to positive changes in every area of our lives."
- Louise Hay

"The greatest discovery in life is self-discovery. Until you find yourself, you will always be someone else. Become yourself."
- Myles Munroe

"I believe if you change the way you look at things, the things you look at change."
- Dr. Wayne Dyer

"What we cannot see, or have not discovered for ourselves becomes difficult to acknowledge."

Thought and reality are experienced based on each perspective. Changing your perspective can change your reality. The reality for one individual is not necessarily the same reality for another. What we cannot see, hear or taste; what we have not discovered for ourselves becomes difficult to acknowledge. My gaining weight was never experienced from another person's perspective. I was not taking action. I wasn't doing the work.

My warped perspective of myself was very different from the pleasant perspective others had of me. I must make a good first impression, then my second…maybe my Donald Duck in Braveheart or Cookie Monster as Joe Pesci's character in Goodfellas, or Goofy as The Terminator. I've got thousands of them.

Your belief system is completely built on your own life experiences and the attachments your BOSS has selected and established. Some experiences have a way of searching for connections and instantly linking root feelings. These feelings are connected to other emotional past experiences. They then initiate the various senses. When you understand your BOSS is YOU, you will be better for it...You may not have all of the updates or upgrades available...yet.

You Have a BOSS:
(Brain Operating Super System)

Like your phone's operating system. You can use an upgrade once in a while. There are many ways to upgrade your BOSS. There are educational options and opportunities all around. Each day your BOSS updates with whatever new data has entered the system. That could be fun data, but that could be unpleasant data.

Nonetheless, more stuff has to be logged in, designated, rated, and then filed away under various files that can cross and connect to an unlimited group of files your BOSS has already created, developed, and built over your entire lifetime.

I found the biggest problem with my BOSS was that it had created files that are still being used and have been outdated since the turn of the century. That's when I updated and began working on my upgrade.

Your brain can do things that you cannot even comprehend.

As we move further along in this book, we will touch upon the question: What makes an improviser so comfortable with having no plan? What makes that jazz musician know his freestyle, flavor, and oddly blended notes will work? He or She just does.

They trust in the fact that they've put in the time and effort to build their knowledge and skill set to the level of mastery.

Your BOSS is no different than anyone else's. On any day you can upgrade your system. You can reset the way you think about things. Instead of thinking of the mistake you made earlier; obsessing over what happened. Keyword…Happened. It's done.

Move forward. Any moment spent beyond the initial emotions and feelings coming up is wasted time and thought.

Instead of concentrating on what food I am going to eat when I get out of work? I now typically plan it and know before that time comes. This removes the slippery slope possibilities from the equation. I also just envision a healthier me and I consciously and constantly ask myself…does that food choice support me being healthy? If not, it is not on my menu…most of the time.

You can download new processes that will help you increase your performance levels. If you were in a business that exists by getting others to buy in. What are they buying? It could be YOU, your product, your service, your opinion, or even your request for a first date. We're all Selling IT in some way. In many occupations, people do not even realize that they rely on their performance too.

When we are conscious, we perform better. When we are focused, we perform better. People who live high-performance lifestyles get high-performance results.

Think about it like this. In a race between a 2024 Lamborghini Revuleto and a 1973 Ford Pinto, who'd you bet on? I am betting that you would agree that the level of performance between the two is obvious. The Lambo would win by a landslide, but once in a while the Pinto would be rebuilt. This is no bum of a car. Maybe this Pinto now has a 426 Racing Hemi with fully injected nitrous and a supercharger to top it off. Proving the adage you never know what's under the hood, or don't judge a Pinto by its cover.

Constantly Upgrade Your BOSS! Let it do the Work

When your BOSS is working like a well-oiled machine, the wind is at your back. You're winning in some way every day. YOU are losing the weight YOU wanna lose. YOU are having great pitches leading to locking in the client you've had on the hook for months. She finally says yes to going out to dinner with you…as long as you wear pants.

As you realign your BOSS file system, delete old files that have no use for you anymore. By challenging the thought and overwriting it with the new thought based in today's reality, not yesterday's old news and outdated childhood beliefs. You can sever those well-rooted connections between older files and new input. Let go of that shit!

I promise you this, if you have faith to hear me out. I am a guy who does what I say, says what I want and need, and lives in a state of comfort. This allows happiness to manifest in my life often and in amazing ways.

My BOSS was primarily working with certain files that were based on forced beliefs and built on top of a weak foundation. By upgrading my Brains Operating Super System, I have been able to make unbelievable adjustments, rebuild my entire thought processing system, checked off everything on my childhood bucket list, and much more. Well, there was one event that was not on my bucket list. My best pals made me wear a gold lamé speedo and pushed me out of the back of a van. I had to chase after them to get back in, this happened in Times Square NYC. It's been checked off the list.

94

Let's open the hood, turn on your DO switch, and click the .exe file in your head to begin the upgrade (Congratulations! You already started when you opened this book).

I'd like to illustrate the effectiveness of my B.O.S.S. system with a specific situation where it proved invaluable for me. It was a make-up an instant joke game called 185.

185

There's a game called 185. It's an interesting game because you are forced to create a joke out of thin air. You're given the format and the audience gives you the word for the joke to jump off with.

The format goes like this:

185 _____'s walk into a bar. The Bartender says: "We don't serve _____'s here. The _____'s reply "Why not?" The bartender replies _____ (Punchline).

One day an audience member yelled out "TRUCKS!" I thought to myself, I know nothing about trucks, but as nobody was moving, I stepped forward and began to tell the joke…

…FLASHBACK to 1976'ish about a half century ago. I was in elementary school, and I'm sitting on the school bus next to a boy named Scotty. We were on our way to school. I'd say it was 4th maybe 5th grade. Sometimes Scotty and I would get along, sometimes we did not. Scotty had some behavioral issues and liked to pick his nose and eat it…Yummy. I was a wise ass.

Scotty was taller and heavier than probably all of the kids on that bus, but that did not stop the kids from teasing him…a lot, and he got angry very easily. Sometimes I would get teased too, but I also had a hair trigger, reacting on impulse problem. After a few scuffles on the bus, my abuse abated. So, when those same douchey kids kept on messing with Scotty, I didn't like it. Having experienced this all too much, I felt compassion. I didn't like having to listen to them argue, or see him so upset and angry. Even though he was definitely not my favorite person back then, I always tried to keep the bus seat next me open for him. This way we would keep each other amused and not get abused. Now, imagine going to a School 35 minutes away from your house, but with stopping to pick up kids all the way, it was an hour plus on a bus to school and then again home from school. And this was no regular school. It was a special school for children with learning disabilities. I spent two hours in a school bus every day with Scotty and kids just like me.

Scott loved to talk about where his dad went and what his dad was doing that day. His dad was a big rig truck driver. He would tell me all about trucks, all about the names of the big rig trucks. Mack trucks, Peterbilt trucks and last but not least a brand that I always thought was called Kennelsworth, but now know it's actually Kenworth Trucks. Who knew? Who cared?

Now this is information that I have no use for today and if it wasn't for Scotty, I would never have known those three names. Without any doubt, I can tell you that I have not thought about Scotty or 18 wheelers in at least 45 years.

The point of the story is the brain is able to deliver what is needed when we need it, and it happens in an instant!

There you have the back story of my wonderful relationship with Scotty and how this truck info, I never thought had any value or would ever use in my life; how this morsal POPPED in with what turned out to be valuable information. It had been stored away in the dark recesses of my mind. Somehow this information suddenly arrived in the moment …that 185 moments.

Deep in your brain, imagine there are rows and rows in rooms and rooms of filing cabinets. Those cabinets store all of the memories, experiences, senses, etc. Some files are never tapped again and fade with time. Others create attachments like the time you fell off your bicycle and received the scar on your elbow…or when you had that very pretty young teacher, who asked you to stand up in the exact same moment you were imagining her naked in your swimming pool. You know there is no way you can really follow that instruction. You're thinking "Um…I can't stand up! Theres something happening in my pants. I do not understand or care to exhibit this new stiffening pup tent forming in my pants for the entire class to see. Or, perhaps that time you gambled on a fart, and lost. Every single incident is documented and banked in one of those file cabinets.

There are times when your brain finds an unused file that you never remembered or had any clue that tidbit of knowledge would ever be of value or needed for anything. The coolest part is that your brain does it faster than a fraction of a fraction of a second. It's as if the universe (or G-d if you wish) just throws you what you need in the moment.

This is something we all have the capability of doing, but we rarely allow ourselves to trust it. Again, the thinking gets in the way.

This particular 185 experience changed my way of thinking about how I think and how amazing the human brain works. I am not a doctor. I am not a scientist, but as a Neuro diverse improviser, I can tell you with clear conviction of fact. My brain and your brain are capable of doing things that we cannot even comprehend.

So, back to that night on the stage and my 185 joke.

AUDIENCE MEMBER
Trucks

1…2…3…second's pass. In my head → Come on somebody Go!

Uh oh…Ughh…nobody is stepping out…well…OK, here goes…I step up to the microphone…apprehensively. I had nothing. I was willing to die on my sword and fail to give the others time to come up with something.

ME
185 Trucks Walk into a bar.
The bartender says we don't serve trucks here,
and the trucks replied "Why not?"
The bartender says…uh…"we just don't. That's the rule."
So, the trucks said …um…
(at this point I've still got nothing)
"…Ah,don't worry Mack…My buddy Peterbilt this place
and I'm wondering, how much is this Kenilworth".

The moment that came out of my mouth, I was astonished. Where in the world did that come from? It's been almost a half century since I saw Scotty, or thought about the name of a big rig truck. But, for some reason, my brain was able to access usable information in a flash. Information that has been filed away and had no use since downloading it in the 70's.

Why am I telling you this story? Because that was the moment that I truly recognized my own ability and the amazing things a human brain can do beyond our own understanding. I was not thinking about it, it just came to me when I needed it.

Today I trust my gut instincts. Today I know that the answers will come to me. I just have to stay present, be conscious and simply listen.

Trust your mind to deliver what you need. Answers and truth are at your fingertips. Listen to that voice that tells you instantly. Then ignore or disregard that inner critic voice that seems to creep in to tell us we are not good enough or we can't do it. Doing its best to knock you off track or keep you down.

Power of Fast Paced Learning

In life and the fast-paced world of business, time is of the essence. We don't always have the luxury of traditional learning methods. Non-traditional methods can work too. I once had a teacher that used a yardstick to whip your butt. Literally. It became a rite of passage for Mr. Chicco to hit you with Big Bertha. Yup, it had a name. He would be in jail for that today, but in all honesty, it always got the kid's attention and, in my case, I did better in his class. I can also confess that he asked me if I was OK with taking the shots from Big Bertha. I didn't know you had the choice before he would break out the torture stick. In truth, it did not really hurt at all. The sound it made was much louder than the ouch. I in no way condone this type of non- traditional teaching method...I use duct tape.

As we connect with people in our business lives, we rarely truly know what makes our new audience tick. Some might love to talk about themselves, or want you to just get to the numbers, "How much will this cost me?" Others will love your stories and tangents.

It takes some time to know exactly who your perfect audience may be. This can often take years to yield results. That's where IT steps in.

Participating in Quick Wit, Brain Shaking, and Improvisational exercises are the express lanes of learning. They help increase your mental agility to adapt to the unplanned and change quickly. To better comprehend and focus on only what is happening right now. When you are better able to think on your feet, you will respond confidently, creatively, and effectively to the unexpected twists and turns of your home life and business landscape.

Whether it's a sudden client meeting or an impromptu presentation. Even when asking for a raise, a discount, or being calm, confident, and cool when asking the 6'8" 350+ lb. biker standing in front of you on line to please get his service dog to stop assaulting you and let go of your leg.

You are now ready to face these events head-on. Armed with the skills of an improviser, you'll have Bluto smiling, apologizing for Fido's lude and lascivious behavior, and paying for the bottle of champagne you are holding to celebrate a win!

Performance Doesn't Only Happen on The Stage: Likeability

Likeability is paramount in selling it. Your likeability level increases unsolicited opportunities. When someone you've just met likes you, that stranger may ask you what you do to make a living. You talk about many things beyond just work stuff. Because they now like you, a week later you get a surprise client showing up on your cell phone, email box, or your actual doorstep. It's always nice to have that new project, due to another referral from one of the many people who like you. When a comedian steps on stage, they have moments before the audience determines their Likability Level. Opening strong and closing strong is a must for success.

Everyone is Performing or Selling "IT" in Some Way

Any successful Leader, Teacher, CEO, Speaker, Therapist, Realtor, Trainer, Manager, Writer, Front Desk Clerk, Customer Service Rep, plus so many other careers, and in everyday life. YOU ARE PERFORMING TO AN AUDIENCE! Life is a performance. In any situation you need to get someone to buy into your idea, service, your product, your opinion, or simply just win someone over, to persuade someone (presentations, seminars, instructing, or selling), do not kid yourself. YOU ARE

PERFORMING TO AN AUDIENCE!

You want them to approve your plan, develop your concept, creation, idea, buy your product, or even just say yes when you ask someone out for a date...and again when you are on that first date...YOU ARE PERFORMING TO AN AUDIENCE!

Whether it is a large group, a small group or even an audience of just one, it's an edge to have the skills and confidence in your abilities to win them over before you ever walk into that room or pick up that phone. This is paramount if you want them to say yes, to agree with you...to marry you.

The most successful leaders (from entrepreneurs, and business owners to CEOs, etc....) they are all adept at performing in front of people and their teams. Do you want to be the best performer you can be?

In What Way Do You Perform

Exercise – In what way do you perform? Where in your life are you communicating intending to sell it? For years, it was my bullshit. Now as you can see, I'm selling a process, some hope, some motivation, and hopefully a couple of laughs and smiles. I'm trying to get something from customer service. I'm selling them to give me what I want. Whether you are selling it on the phone or at work. To your employees, your kids, your teacher, your potential client, etc.

What is your "it"? How do you sell it? Where are you selling it? To whom are you selling it? Do your best to list three areas in your life that in some way you had to get someone else to buy in on your product, your service, your opinion, your direction, your decoration style, your request, your choice of restaurant, and no, not sushi again.

"Hey kiddo, go throw out the garbage. If not, there is a very strong possibility I might put you up for adoption." Do you think the kid took the garbage out? I sold it, he bought it. Now drop and give me three!

Trusting in Faith or the Universe: Believe What YourGut Tells You

Selling is often about making quick decisions and trusting your instincts. We'll start by discussing the power of trusting yourself, your gut feelings, and even having faith in the universe to guide you. Learn to let go of self-doubt and trust your gut, your inner compass when navigating the sales world. You'll often find yourself making decisions on the fly. You might wonder, how can you navigate this uncertain terrain? The answer lies in trust – trust in yourself, in your ability to think of something on the spot, and your natural instincts. You know your shit! Trust in your abilities.

Every successful salesperson has a well-honed gut feeling. It's a sixth sense developed through experience, practice, and intuition. When you trust your instincts, you're more likely to make quick, informed decisions that can win over customers.

Additionally, consider the power of faith – not just in a higher power but in the universe's ability to guide you. Trust that things will work out, even if you can't see the entire path. Embrace uncertainty as an opportunity, not a hindrance. In the world of improvisation, there are no scripts, only the faith that the next line will come naturally.

So, as we move forward in this chapter, remember that you possess the inner compass that can lead you to unscripted success. Trust your instincts, have faith in yourself, and embrace the unpredictable nature of sales. You're perfect exactly the way you are, and your uniqueness is your greatest asset.

The human BOSS knows it all. It maintains every file in your virtual life library. It's your thinking machine. You can close your eyes and go back to a special memory, it gets loaded and like a time machine, the mind can travel backward through time...or create and imagine the future. You can go anywhere in a split second. Let's try this simple exercise for a moment just for you to personally solidify what I mean by this.

With your eyes closed, let's go back to the first memory you have. Now, move to around 13 ... then up to another clear memory from your past. You would be surprised to know that the brain waves that are creating the memory, are nearly identical to the actual live recording. It is as if you are truly there. You cannot touch it, but you can bring up feelings that existed at the time your database recorded it.

Now let's go into the future. It's your future, 1st Rule You must think of a positive outcome only; a wish list (within logical reason to start). This is your exercise and it must be a happy creation.

Think fast! What was it like? Were you able to send your imagination to a positive experience and stay there, or did an inner critic crash the party? If not just now, in the past? The self-doubting thoughts manifest into feeling like poop. It's always okay to take a moment to time travel or daydream if you wish. When it moves beyond a moment, it becomes fantasy land and sucks precious seconds, minutes, hours, days, years, and in my case, decades of life that cannot be regained. Time is an enormously important commodityin my life. I know I will only get so many minutes in this life.

The same goes for wasting valuable time choosing to $pend those minutes, hours, days, years, or again, like me, decades doing things that would bring nothing of value in return. An unnecessary argument, you're taking your finger (save your thumbs from carpal tunnel. It sucks!) and swiping up ^ down v left

< right > watching cat videos. Ok, they are pretty irresistible, but come on. Go take a walk instead.

Meet My Life Coach L.A.R.R.Y.

On or Off-track - Alignment or   Mis-alignment

When I have a goal, I find it hard to stay centered if I'm in my head. It's hard to stay on track, to reach that goal without having unforeseen distractions. That's natural and part of life, but if I go off track, my entire process gets thrown out of alignment. When I am not aligned with my goals or my purpose for doing what I'm doing, I don't feel as comfortable. I don't do as well in whatever task I'm doing. I could easily lose my way and go so far off track that it's hard to find the path again. That's why I have my friend Larry. Yes, I know it's corny, but the truth is, I have been using Larry as my life coach and I gotta tell you he's a lot cheaper and helps me get the value out of myself. He helps me keep organized which helps my neurodiverse hyper-aware brain remember and keep order in my life in general.

I've worked with a few life coaches, but regardless of who it was, I was still fat, uncomfortable in my own skin, and not very happy. It was only when LARRY showed up that everything changed. This was a process I was writing down for use in my coaching and in mentoring others with Hyper-Awareness or ADHD if you must. I was writing down a list of the top five things that I've done to help me reach the physical and mental sense of comfortable success I had hoped to achieve for decades. Science has proven writing down a goal increases your completing that goal by 42%. Those odds sound too good to be true. They are not. Go look it up…I just did.

Lists - Alarms - Reminders - Repetition - YES! The list started with…Lists, Alarms, and Reminders. List - Alarms -

104

Reminders

I hadn't seen him yet. Then I thought it is not just using these helpful tools every day, it is repeating them over and over again, so I added...**R**epetition.

It was then that he caught my eye. I have a couple of friends named Larry, and I call them LARR. It was just screaming for me to find a word that started with a **Y**. Obviously, there was only one option to go with. C'mon, Say it with me! **Y**es!!!

We've already gone over why saying Yes has so much more power than a No. Plus, it helps to remember the concept of Yes, and...

Lists keep me aware of what I want to get done and the things I need to get done. I usually put my "To Do" list in order of priority and I use the notes app on my phone. I use the little check-off bubbles right next to each event task. This way when it's been completed, I tap that circle - "Bloop! - and it drops to the end of the list; sitting pretty with the other full circles. Done. Ha! Look at that, I've just completed something. Yay for me. I would call that a win. Winning feels good.

Alarms help me stay on time. I have about 50 pre-sets per week. Alarms have always been the best tool I have to remind me to do things every day, every week. I set an alarm for everything important to me. It can be as simple as "Go get gas on the way home".

Reminders are necessary for my hyper-aware brain to remember what is not top of mind. The best part of setting multiple reminders on the calendar in advance is those events or other important matters I may have completely forgotten about. They pop up for me every morning as I do not get ahead of my daily reality. Now, I do prepare by using my to-do lists, alarms, and my calendar. Right Now!

Hey Adam, can you come over and help me with a new project I'm starting up?". "Ok, when?" "Friday at 5:30ish?" "Done." "And, please do not wear a tube top again." The end. I immediately enter it into my calendar and add three reminders for that event. 1 week, 1 day, and 1 hour. Is it overkill? Yes. It takes maybe an extra 20 seconds I'm willing to spend, but it is off my plate instantly. When that time is near, my neurodiverse brain will not have to worry if I get caught up and don't remember. I will be ready.

Repetition reinforces these new habits. By repeating these steps, you will be better prepared, ahead of time, for those things that are important to you (and those you love). Repeating an action will help solidify a routine that works best for you.

If you have ever played Super Mario Bros, you know first, you are going to lose life after life, over and over again. Each time you learn what does work, and what does NOT work. By repeating the level, you recall hazards and know when that turtle is going to pop up out of that green pipe/tube whatever it is.

Yes, you can! **YES!**

Ask? Ask, Away!

I find when there's something that I want or something that I want to do that's going to take someone else to help make that happen. I always look to see who's in my tribe that could have some connection to this desired result.

Asking questions and observing others is how we learn most of what we know. Asking others for something you want is not always so simple. For some reason, we get caught up in the mindset of "What if they say no?" or "That's just not the way it's done" or maybe "I wonder if they can smell that one?"

One thing I can guarantee is this. If you do not take that step or risk facing that rejection, if you DO NOT open your mouth and ask for it, nothing will happen. That is a fact.

Another fact is, if by chance you DO open your mouth and YOU ask for it, you may have nothing happen. Or, you can get exactly what you want. Know how to answer any question smarter. They will appreciate the honesty and respect you for it.

If you don't know the answer don't try to fake it. When we do, lacking an answer shows you may not be prepared and it may be evident that you are scrambling. It would always be better to frame the answer to best fit you. OR be truthful by saying: I am not completely sure of the answer so, let me do some research, and educate myself I will get back to you ASAP. Sometimes you can answer the question by steering your answer towards your focused path with a left turn and a fun story.

Here's a fun story that truly shows how asking for something can turn into something well beyond your dreams.

I walked into an audition and another actor, someone I always enjoy talking to in the waiting rooms smiles wide, and says, "Hey, Congratulations!" I was confused. My child was born six months ago and I've seen him a couple of times so not knowing what he was talking about I said "Uh, what for?" He proceeded to tell me that I won the NAVGTR award.

I was shocked!? A) I've never heard of a NAVGTR award and B) I had no idea I was even nominated for one. He told me that it was one of the more prestigious awards in the Voice-Over video game business. It stands for National Association of Video Game Testers, and Reviewers. I was excited because, in all honesty, I didn't know what game it was that I had won for. I worked on a few games that year.

When I got home, I looked up this association and picked up the phone. When I got someone on the other line, they were happy to hear from me. I was beyond excited to find out that they were sending me a trophy and told me who I was up against.

Turns out, it was not a group of scrubs. I was shocked to find out my fellow nominees were Sir Patrick Stewart, as Professor X in the X-Men video game. Christopher Lee as Count Doku in a Star Wars video game. Terrence Stamp, and one other person I cannot recall. Did I win? Yes, I did!

Ask and you shall receive

...FLASHBACK: It's about a year earlier. I was at casting call for a new video game. I was given the role of Khelgar Iron Fist to read. The copy was fun. He was a little warrior. I chose to do a Scottish warrior accent. I was very confident I'd nail it.

Before I was called into the room, I saw the copy and character breakdown for another character on the table. I picked it up, it was for a character called the King of Shadows. The breakdown explained that this was the boss of all bosses, and the last and most fierce battle in the game. The description included the line, The King is Death Incarnated. Oooo that kind of voice sounds yummy.

Typically, you go in for the role you've been called in on and you leave. Asking the Casting Director is pretty much frowned on. The preferred way would be for me to call my agent and have them ask the Casting Director for another slot to give that character a run.

This audition happened at a time in my life when I was challenging anything and everything that limited me, censored or restricted my ideas, words, and most of all, my thoughts. I was challenging myself in those moments. I would feel like a coward NO MORE!

I started asking for what I wanted or what I needed in many areas of my life. I was working hard against that self-doubt, told that inner critic to F#@&' off, and began chipping away at a lifetime of scattered false beliefs, and habits.

As the door opened, the actor reading before me came out of the door with a wide smile on his face. The assistant casting director was right behind him and followed him out. She picked up the clipboard and looked at the sign-in sheet. Adam Seitz (it was spelled wrong on her call list).

When I walked into the room, I was thrown off for a moment, I was surprised to see a row of producers, and the director sitting on both sides of the camera staring at me.

Judy introduced me, that's Judy Henderson. She is one of the best casting directors out there, and yes, she is another amazing Judy. I gave them my best Khelgar and just as Judy said, thank you Adam, I went for it. I asked her in front of all those bigwigs if it would be okay for me to give them a quick run for the King of Shadows. She froze for a second not wanting to disappoint me, but also knowing she had a room full of actors waiting to come in after me. She paused for a moment and took a quick scan to read the room. Luckily for me what she saw was the agreeable faces of the producers and director nodding their approval.

Fast forward I got a call from my agent telling me that I just booked…Khelgar! I was excited and kind of bummed that I did not get the King of Shadows. When I went in to the studio to record my character, I ended up finishing all of my lines way sooner than the time they had allotted. They were paying me, so they wanted to get as much bang for their buck, and I was more than happy to provide what they needed.

Then the Director said "You know what? Why don't you give us a read on the King of Shadows." Glory! They had no idea that I was jumping for joy like Snoopy doing his happy dance. I looked the lines very quickly, and away we went. I ended up finishing him fairly quickly too so they had me read for two other characters. In total, they got four voices out of me and I had a blast playing with them in the studio for a few days.

Fast forward back to the moment, I hung up the phone call with the folks at the NAVGTR awards. This is where it gets even wilder. I decided to call Judy. Would you believe I won an award for that game? You did?! That's fantastic. As we finished our conversation she said: What are you doing this weekend? I said whatever you need me to do, why what's up? She told me that she had a reading over the weekend, there was no pay, and she would like me to look at a role. She said I was thinking about you for the Lord and Taylor Guy. I was up for anything so she sent me the script and the breakdown. It was Neil Simon's "Barefoot in the Park".

I opened the script and found the Lord and Taylor guy. The role only had three words, and those three words were yelled out from offstage.

LORD & TAYOR DELIVERY MAN
"Lord and Taylor!"

The line was smaller than the character's name. The role is all visual humor. It seemed fun, but I saw there was another character in that scene, I said wow that would be a fun role. This was the telephone repair man. It just so happened they made a movie based on the original Broadway production with Jane Fonda and Robert Redford. The Telephone Repair Man was played by the same man who did the Broadway production. His name, Herbie Edelman. I remembered that name because he was a good friend of my father's. At this point, my dad was already gone, but I remember him talking about Herb anytime we'd see him on a show or in a movie. I could only imagine playing that larger role instead. I liked that role a lot more than the Lord and Taylor guy.

She had asked me to get back to her to let her know if I could handle it. I did get back to her and I said "I could handle the Lord and Taylor guy". She said great we're all set then I'll see you on Saturday. I then took a breath and ASKED AWAY… "um, Judy do you have anyone for the telephone repair man?" She said I'm supposed to, but I'm not sure if he'll do it or not. I'm waiting to find out. So…I ASKED her if there was any chance that I could audition to read for that role in the reading instead. She said there is no audition. It's only a reading. A moment later, Judy said, "You know what, he was supposed to get back to me by early this morning and I haven't heard from him yet. So YES, you can do the telephone repair man, but beforehand you will have to meet the Director first so he can approve it! Holy shit! I am going to meet the Director.

So, I set up an appointment. The timing was perfect because I had to come into the city that day for a commercial callback anyway. It's that day my wife and my baby girl came with me for the ride. We decided we'd have a nice day out in the city after the audition and the meeting with the Director. When I came downstairs from the callback, I noticed a parking ticket on the windshield. I did not see my wife or the baby. I was pretty clear "Please do not get out of the driver seat because if you do, they can ticket or tow the car". Where is she?

I looked both ways, and I realized the back of the Explorer was open. She is changing a diaper. She had no idea there was a ticket on the car. She must have been ticketed when she began changing the diaper. The cop giving out tickets must not have seen her. We could see it was printed only three minutes ago. No cop on site? We read the ticket...WHAT? Just great. I gave a $185.00 f#@%ing gift to the city of NY for the privilege of cleaning up baby shit.

So, we're on our way to meet the Director. I'm not in the happiest mood now because I'm gonna have to take time off and go to a traffic court in New York City, but I still looked over my script and got ready while my wife drove to the director's office. I gave her and the baby a kiss. She told me to go break a leg and I went in.

Standing in the hallway after knocking on the door several times, I am now completely dripping in sweat. The Director is not there. No one is answering his door at all, and I'm in the hallway that has to be 120°. As I'm about to give up and just go downstairs to cool off. I say where the F' is this man? At that exact moment, Scott Elliot came around the corner, looked at me, and said "That Fu@%ing man is right here. He took one look at me and in shock he said "Oh my God, you're dripping! Please come in. Let me give you some cold water.

When we went in. I immediately thought of "Taking the scenic route". Before he could say anything about the show, I jumped right into the fact that I just got a ticket while my wife was in the back of the Explorer changing the diaper. He said that is so effing evil. I explained she didn't see the officer, and the officer didn't see her yada yada yada.

Before I could pull out the script to go over whatever he wanted to go over with me, he stopped me and said "I can tell you are funny. I'll see you tomorrow at 2:30". I pushed the script back down into my back pocket, said thank you, got up, and walked out of the room. This was pretty cool. I felt it went OK.

The next day, I walked into the building. I find the room number and when I walk in, I see another talented actor I knew who had the good fortune of getting to read for the Lord and Taylor guy that day. Within moments, Tony Roberts walked into the room, and then Jill Clayburgh walks into the room; followed by Patrick Wilson and the lovely Amanda Peet. Scott came in and we went over it and did a full read-through with just us in the room. It went very well. They said to take a one-hour break to grab something to eat and we would do it again in an hour.

Patrick and I went to grab lunch at Chipotle (my first ever, yum). What was interesting was that I had no idea who Patrick was. I thought he was just another young handsome actor doing a reading. Nope. It turns out Patrick has been on Broadway for quite a while already. He was in The Full Monty, All my Sons, and what is so ironic, he played Curly in Oklahoma the day I decided that Broadway could be achievable.

After the two-block walk back and being stopped three times for selfies and autographs (not for me, obviously), we got back to the rehearsal hall. As we went back and entered the room there was nobody there. We did hear some voices further down the hall, so we walked that way. When we walked into the room, I was surprised to see it was filled with people in suits and a large table in the middle. Scott, the Director was there with a wide smile welcoming us back. As I scanned the room, I got a bit nervous. That is until an older man moving slowly with a cane walked in. As he looked up, I saw the face of Neil Simon. Holy cannoli!

I was very excited to perform his words, and possibly even meet him. Another familiar face walked in, but I couldn't place it. I leaned over to Amanda or Jill and asked "Who is that?" It was the eccentric and funny fashion designer Issac Mizrahi. The room settled and we began the reading. I opened it up with Amanda, and we got great laughs. I then sat there and watched the room while the others finished Act 1. We had a brief intermission, and Amanda and I opened Act 2 again. We totally killed it! Big hearty, deep from the gut, loud happy laughs. I loved every second.

As we ended, I fought the urge to hang out too long afterward. I got some nice feedback, said thank you, and left. As I walked towards the elevator, I saw Neil standing in front of three steps. He looked like he was not comfortable stepping without a little help.

Neil's Assistant had made a pit stop in the ladies' room, and not wanting to stand there, he decided to navigate the step(s) on his own. I came up and said "Would you like a human handrail? Steps are tough for me too." (Remember I am over 400lbs at the time). I assisted him and let him know that I knew of the guy who played the role on Broadway and in the movie, he said "Yes Herbie", I said that's right. We spoke for about a minute and we went our separate ways. Walking back to my car, a huge wave of gratitude hit me. I had loved this man's plays and movies for my entire life.

FIRETRUCK MOMENT: Interesting side note, Herbie was a cab driver when he was cast by Mike Nichols to play Murray the Cop in Neil's Tony award winning play, The Odd Couple. The show and Herbie moved on to the film which earned a couple of Academy Award nominations. Then onto TV history winning multiple Emmy Awards. Not sure any piece of theater had such a run of success on all three entertainment mediums. It is still one of my favorite TV shows of all time. It was also, ironically, running on Broadway at the same time that I was doing Barefoot. This man in his late 80s had TWO Broadway revivals running at the same time 40 years later. This particular coincidence played a big role later on the down the road.

Great acting story sidenote: Al Molinari was cast by Garry Marshall to play the role of Murray on the TV series. Herb went on to marry Bea Arthur on the Golden Girls. Al was fortunate to not only step into that iconic role, but when Pat Morita left to do his show "Mr. T & Tina, Al also stepped in and took over as Al Delveccio, the owner of Arnolds on Happy Days. Pat's show lasted one month before it was canceled.

Fast forward to the following Monday. I called the casting office and before I spoke to Judy, another fantastic casting director, Kim Graham, answered the phone:

> KIM
> HI Adam. Have you heard from Roy yet?

> ME
> Who's Roy?

> KIM
> Hold on Judy wants to talk to you,
> and I didn't say anything.

Judy got on the phone and asked me the same question.

> JUDY
> Hi Adam. Has Roy called you yet?

> ME
> (Again)
> Roy Who?

It was at this moment that I received some of the coolest news I have ever received.

> JUDY
> Roy Gabay. Please tell your manager to expect his call.
> Cause…Adam, they're making you an offer.

> ME
> An offer? For what?

JUDY
They want you for the show.

ME
What show?

JUDY
Um, the show we just did the reading for silly.
Barefoot in the Park?!

ME
(Shocked)
No way! Are you serious?

JUDY
(I could clearly hear her smiling)
Yes, I am.

ME
Wow! Where are they doing it?

JUDY
Broadway.

Silence.

ME
What?

JUDY
Broadway!

ME
Holy Shit! I thought you said,
"It was just a reading?"

116

JUDY

It was. Who do you think all those people in the room were watching? They were all there to see it so we could, hopefully, get them to produce it. They loved it! They loved you, and they are producing it!

ME

Judy, do you know I've never done a play in my entire life?

JUDY

(That takes a moment to register) Well…wait…WHAT?

ME

I was a comedian. I did a lot of Improv and stand-up comedy, but not in a theater like that.

JUDY

I don't believe it.

ME

Nope. I fell into this business when I did a few commercials.

JUDY

Didn't you do a play in school?

ME

Nope, I was a production guy, I got a couple of jobs on TV, Film, Cartoons, and Video Games. One of which YOU booked me on, and they just gave me that award for.

JUDY

Wow.

ME

Other than my stand-up material, I've never been in a scripted, live staged show before.

JUDY
Ok…Well…DO NOT tell that to anyone.
Keep it to yourself.

I got off the phone. I called my mom first and I called my wife, then my sisters, and then my manager who told me she was about to call me. She just got a phone call from a guy named Roy.

The moral of the story is to ask for what you want.

- If I did not ask to read for the King of Shadows, I don't know if I would've impressed that group enough to cast me.
- If I did not ask, I would never have won that NAVGTR award.
- If I didn't ask, I would never have called Judy to tell her I won the award.
- If I didn't ask, I would've never been Harry Pepper, the telephone repair man. In fact, I would have been a reader of the Lord and Taylor guy. A role I would have never booked.

FIRETRUCK MOMENT: That role went to an amazing Man (and my Cort theater roommate) in his mid-60s from Trinidad Tobago named Sulivan Walker. He took those three words, from off stage, and made his actions and physicality new all the time. Brilliant and funny. He got many applause breaks without ever opening his mouth on the stage. He has passed now, but you can still see him in great movies like The Firm, Crocodile Dundee, and Get Rich or Die Trying. A great example of there are never any small roles in a show. Every role has a purpose.

- If I didn't ask, I would never have had my Broadway debut.
- If I didn't ask, I would never have been seen in that show and asked to audition for the show that became my second Broadway show, "Talk Radio".

118

- If I didn't ask, I would've never been seen by Joe Mantello (the Director of that revival of the Odd Couple)
- If I didn't ask, Joe would never have asked me to do a reading for his next Broadway show. That became my third Broadway show in three years.

If you DO NOT ask, nothing happens.

If you DO ask…nothing may still be the result, but by asking you open up a door of possibility, a YES, and another win!

Don't hesitate! Ask away. You may get to play.

Setting Goals

Set realistic and far-out wishful goals…Writing them down and setting a due date along with the undesirable (or embarrassingly self-deprecating yet funny to others) consequence. (e.g. Clown nose for a day, Shave your head, pie to the face by a stranger).

"Ideas without actions are worthless"
~ Helen Keller

Exercise:

- *Make a list of the things you need done on a daily basis.*
- *Make a list of new, recent, and current goals that are at the front of the line for you.*
- *Make a list of where you want to be in 5 years and what you want to achieve long term.*
- *Make a list of what you've wanted to get done, but haven't started or finished yet.*

Out of the Box? What Box?

My Dad was fantastic at getting what he wanted. He would find creative ways to get the job done or to make sure when the show must go on, it did…and so much more.

After my dad was gone, I wanted to know as much as I could about how he ran the business. At this point, I had no idea I would be in charge so early in my life. I spoke to so many of his friends and colleagues and heard some fantastic stories. When they say, sometimes you gotta work out of the box or on the edge, maybe even stretch it to the limit, Seymour Lloyd Sietz was a master.

Back in the early 70s, there was a producer who was hoping to get his event on broadcast television. My dad knew the people you would need to know on several networks. He also knew the world of syndication and advertising.

Being an entrepreneur, Dad preferred ownership versus partnership. He knew how to weigh risk versus reward and successfully capitalized in many amazing ways.

That producer didn't know how to get a television show on the air. That's why he came to Dad, this was the story he told me. This particular show had quite a bit of appeal to it. Dad felt if he could come to the table with it being completely sold out of commercial inventory before the show was to even air, how could any network say no?

He didn't get many instant No's. His no's sounded more like, "Seymour, thanks for the opportunity. I will talk to my team and let you know".

My father had huge balls. I don't know about his testicles; I just know he had nerves. He walked into a major conglomerate. Yes. He would just call or walk in. For instance, when he went to a meeting in any skyscraper, he would stop for a moment before entering the elevator. He would look at the building's directory of companies, the floors they are on, and their room #'s, and write them down. When he was finished with the intended visit, he would stop into every company he had written down earlier. He had a way of simply asking for help with something he needed or wanted, and he'd get it. If he saw it and wanted it, he would ask for it, and in many cases, he would get it. He could schmooze any gatekeeper into opening the gates and connecting him with the decision-maker. He'd then create and close another deal, or three before leaving the building.

Back to the producer in need of Dad's help. Dad walked into the Mega-Corp and said he had this show that was going to be on broadcast network television. A primetime special!

Before he started offering airtime to the agencies to battle over, he wanted to make an offer. Based on the fact that this was a mega-company, with many brands. He convinced them to take on all available media running commercially during the show…at a discounted rate card. Each commercial break would be filled with spots for their products only. This was a very big company. They had a lot of products. They said yes!

The only issue was he did not have a network deal in any way, shape or form. But what he did have was a television show that had not even been shot yet or had any distribution whatsoever. But this non-existent television show was now completely sold out before he even walked into the door to speak to his friend at the network. When he sat down, he said, let's open the calendar and look for a date. This network executive laughed and said Seymour what do you have for me? He said "I have a two-hour special event that I want to make an annual event with you". He explained how popular he expected this annually televised event to be. There was an opportunity for it to expand into more than one annual event. Oh, and by the way, it's completely sold out

121

commercially. So, in essence we're just buying the time. Are you selling any? He made it clear, it's a now-or-never deal. Dad created leverage where there was none. He walked in confidently. He had no doubts. He knew wherever it ended up, that network would do very well regardless if people watched it or not. It's pre-sold! They worked out the details and agreed to the annual arrangement Dad laid out.

The event producer was blown away by what my father was able to do for him. Dad was also able to take ownership of approximately 12 minutes of the show. He would supply and produce all prize, fashion, and fun on-location segments. He was a pioneer in the product placement biz. That relationship lasted for more than a decade.

There was one other story my father told me. He figured out a way to make two shows for the price of one. To have pulled this one off, the chutzpah of this man was enormous. His likeability level was off the charts. He was handsome, authentically charming, funny, and extremely honorable. I learned so much in the few years I had working side by side.

There was not one industry where he didn't know someone. Starting in his mid-teens, he performed with some of the greats of his era. Many of the people he shared the stage with, or crossed paths with ended up at the top of many facets of the entertainment world. Not surprisingly, he had long-established relationships and close friends all over the industry. He was there to capitalize on this new thing called live television. The concept of an Ad-Man was fairly new. Dad had friends running around, all of the top agencies, and in the halls of network brass (CBS, ABC & NBC). He also had many friends in the advertising world, and remember his comedy partner Barry? He was now a beast in the public relations world. He also had a lot of those friends in the entertainment world from his years as a performer.

Dad had an arrangement with WPIX channel 11, a local station and home of the New York Yankees broadcasts. He was already doing business with the Yankees pre-and post-game shows when he got the rights to do the Miss New York beauty pageant for Miss USA. WPIX was where he made his home for years. After a while, the entire crew and executive team were now friends, not just business partners.

Dad had an idea. He would need many pieces to fall into place to put the puzzle together. Talking to the top brass of WPIX might have slowed the progress of this particular idea, so he chose not to. Being that there was already an entire crew complete gear from lighting to broadcast production trucks the whole shebang, he picked up the phone and called Berry Gordy. Berry was the founder and "The Man" at Motown. He asked Berry if he had any new act(s) that he would like to showcase on a variety show. He would fly them out, pick them up, house them all at the resort, fill them with drinks, and feed them. How could Berry say no? He didn't! Dad got Rick James and Patti Austin to perform on his variety show. It was the first time on TV for both of them. Next, he called one of his other friends at either the Shubert Organization or the Nederlander group. I cannot recall, I didn't really care much about anything other than scheming my way into getting quarters for the pinball game room. I was like a junkie playing pinball and playing this new game. It was the first video game, Pong! So, I had no time to care about these things. All I knew was this man was a Broadway producer. He sent a bunch of cast members to perform some of the numbers from the current show he had running at the time. Dad ended it by calling a few talent agents and bringing in some top comedians, singers, dancers, and other cool variety acts.

Now all that had to happen was they needed to finish shooting the Miss New York Pageant and talk the audience into staying for another two hours to enjoy the live taping of a variety show to be aired across the country.

He shot a second television show at zero cost. He already had an open bar and the food was included. The owners of the resort, also now getting national, not just local coverage were more than happy to supply more than enough rooms at the resort to cover everybody.

He syndicated that show and took us on a vacation to Aruba. When we got home, we had an authentic air hockey table, ping pong table, and a billiards table in our basement.

He did it again a few years later when we ended up in Acapulco and he built us a cool swimming pool.

My father understood that in business, there is not always a straight line to your next project. He found sometimes it was better to draw his own lines. This way, he never had an issue crossing them. He taught me what entrepreneurship truly was. Ownership of your own product is better than just having a piece or having a job. He also showed me how to care about the people that helped him to make it happen.

There wasn't ever a time that he was not willing to schlep, tape down wires, or make some coffee for the cameraman. Everyone always felt included and part of his team. I have done my best to carry on with his morals, kindness, and good humor. I like everyone on my team to know that they can come to me and talk to me about anything they need to and I'll always be fair. I never lead from above. I lead from within. Dad truly lived outside the box. His actions said: Boxes? We don't need no stinking boxes!

Team Development

Innovation and creativity are often stifled in the standard rigid and long-established corporate framework. Many years of commerce and doing business this way or that way are hard to change. For example, let's look at "Robert's Rules of Order". I remember as the new President of my Condo Community Association, I read "Robert's Rules". Yes, they did make sense. Meetings were kept under control, we the board members, were not held captive for hours being sweet talked or abused (more often the latter) by the attending citizens of the community, and at times, we did get some things accomplished.

I had a problem with this formulaic and at times, strict parameters in which the introduction of new ideas and concepts had to follow guidelines set in place by a book written over 135 years ago.

Before I was elected, I was just an audience member. I found myself and many other people leaving these board meetings bored. We often felt we were unheard, unhappy, unimportant, and unfulfilled. By allowing the sitting board members and attending citizens to have the opportunity to speak up in the moment (within reason) the fighting stopped and the meetings became more productive and a lot more enjoyable.

As a comedian in a troupe, it only works when we work together to achieve one simple goal. To entertain. Ego and status can get in the way. If we are all trying to get our joke in, we will step on each other's punchlines or hamper callbacks. Once a group mind is achieved, everyone in the equation typically wins.

Think of a company or a team as a living entity. A lot like a machine, but people are the working parts. As it is inside of a human being, every cell serves a purpose. A sperm cell is different from a brain cell. We, like the cells within us, are all different and yet when we all work together, we create one system.

Good or bad. The better the communication and cooperation of all parts, the better the company, team, machine, and human! Sounds simple right?

It takes hard work, maintenance, and consistency to be healthy and function at peak performance. Working together is better than working alone. Companies with multiple departments working independently of each other could benefit and grow from working or better yet playing together with other departments. Agree or disagree, this is true to me.

Exercising, fueling up well, and establishing a good balance between work and play can help keep any entity working well. Sometimes the machine will still work even though a part or a few parts are not functioning correctly.

When a performing troupe works together the audience can see and feel the cohesion. The likability level is raised. When a salesperson is rigid and scripted, the likability level drops. It is likability that helps close deals, win awards, and even get you a date. When this group unity is broken, the audience can see and feel that too. This lack of synergy is a definite detractor for a client, an audience or even a date.

Harmony

A peaceful harmonious relationship between co-workers is vital to any successful project. When one person in a group is singing out of tune you hear it. It is clearly off. The same thing happens when a team is working out of step. A client can see or sense the harmony or the off-key nature of the relationships they are dealing with. I am not saying that co-workers have to be best friends or even fraternize outside of the workplace, but harmony is crucial to success.

Names Are Important

Remembering someone's name and how they pronounce it is

important. It has always been an issue for me. As a "Hyper-Aware" person, I am often introduced to someone, and within moments, my mind is onto the next thing and I cannot remember their name. I hate this particular failing of mine. I always do my best to repeat the name and try to repeat it at least three times to myself. If there are a few people, I will ping-pong the names in my head. John, Tina, James, and Michael ...Michael, Tina, John and James...James, Michael, John, Tina, etc. At some point, I may even say the names and do this out loud. Yes, it may be awkward, but it may also show them it matters to me. It can be a memorable way to make an immediate impact to a group of now-former strangers. It may even be funnier if you make a fake exit and thank them as a group by giving them all completely different names (joking that not one of the actual names stuck). A pleasure meeting you Tom, George, Angela, and Rachel.

This way, when you do meet again you can:

A. Hopefully greet them by their real name.
B. You can say you cannot remember their name, as they give you the correct name you tell them "No that's not it. Maybe rattle off a few other random names while continuing to deny their true name. End with, I'll remember it eventually" (saying their actual name).
C. If not, whatever name you give them will be acceptable until they correct you themselves. This also works well when you are introducing them to another person. When someone cannot remember my name, I say call me Bob. Easy to remember and to this day many people believe my name is Bob.

"I wish my name was Brian because maybe sometimes people would misspell my name and call me Brain. That's like a compliment and you don't even have to be smart to notice it."
- Mitch Hedberg

Community Common Grounds and Similar Interests

Take your time to get as much information about who you'll be talking to beforehand, List everything. That's what Google is for. Then see if any of those things can be connected to your life and experience. This preparation beforehand will give you a major edge. You'll have a little background on them. They will know very little about you…at the beginning.

If there was anything you found out in their background that does click on a mutual experience, or a similar interest, find a way to incorporate it into your conversation, without giving away any clue to them of your knowing that previously, then let them talk. That is the only part of this method that is a bit fudgy. Meaning that you are manufacturing a common bond. The fact that they don't know this conversation was sparked by the background information you already had in your pocket beforehand doesn't matter, it was a way to jump off the expressway.

This is OK. Because like my father at no point did, I ever lie or ever offer something I could not deliver. All they know is you clicked on being fraternity brothers, a collector of anything Star Wars, or that you both have a mutual love of turtles. Look for any way that you could turn off the main road and enjoy the scenic route. I promise this will help you build Evergreen clients that come back year after year. Enjoy the view.

Teams Like We Players NOT Me Players

It always feels better to be included than to feel like you're on the outside. Certain sensitive aspects of business do need to be kept close to the belt. Common sense will show opportunities for teamwork, true collaboration, individual accountability, and refine a smoother-running machine. If you're a right fielder, no let's say the left fielder is not focused because they're not comfortable with something going on, on their team. He's just hoping the opposing team doesn't hit the ball their way is not a very effective way of protecting your bottom line.

I have seen firsthand the transformation of a large group of individuals based in different areas of a company. It's very interesting to watch the person who handles all maintenance playing with the chief operating officer and shining brightly. Attitudes change, judgments begin to disappear, and unification is easily achieved.

When people enjoy a joyful experience together, a connection, and a bond is created. Smiles were had by all, and as I've said earlier, a smile could be contagious. Whether you're the CEO, executive management, a supervisor, a janitor, or a delivery person. One fact is clear: We all wake up in the morning, experience our day, go home, and repeat. We all get happy. We all get sad.

When we have to spend time together, it's always a better environment and a healthier process, and we truly get to know each other as fellow humans on the same team. Don't lead from above, lead from within.

Be on Your Team, Not Above It

How do you feel when someone who has seniority over you likes to make it clear? Being a subordinate isn't always the first choice for most people. Have you heard the saying "The view from upfront, it's a lot better than the view from behind"? I believe when leaders choose to rule in a manner that sets themselves above others. That is really not the most efficient way to lead.

When I was younger in my late teens, I befriended a group that was a grade and some two grades above me. At first, I was the tagalong, I made them laugh, so they liked to keep me around, but it was established who was the leader of the pack. The pecking order system was in full effect.

As the years moved forward and these friends all moved on to college and university I grew up. Mentally. Physically, and constantly. When my friends would come home for a holiday, the dynamic had to change. No longer was I in a position to feel like a tagalong. I felt confident in who I was and most of these friends saw this without any conversation needed. One friend in particular used to be the Leader of the Pack. He was at the top of the food chain in our friend group. He could be a bit of a dick to people that were not in his circle, but when you did get to know him, you got that that was probably because of his experience with older men e.g., his father, and big brother may not have been so pleasant. So, looking back on it, I believe this was just acting out on that behavior he knows.

Accepting me as an equal was not easy, but I was not willing to take the backseat any more. I did not need to drive, but I wanted to sit shotgun. Not the backseat. The middle? Not a chance. After a wrestling match in my swimming pool got a little more physical than he expected, it was now clear. Adam is no longer a cub; he is also a bear.

I tell this story because the relationship got so much better at that point neither of us had any need to be in control or to have that "I am better" sense in the relationship. This happens with growth, age, and experience.

When a CEO or executive staff member chooses to set a pecking order based on negativity rather than an equal playing field. As teammates, he does himself a disservice. I look at it like this, leadership is led by the managers and the pitchers, but they need every player in every position to succeed. I'm not saying that the boss shouldn't still hold the red pencil, and make the final decision, but opening up the conversation to the entire team can yield some surprising results.

Play together - Play more

Go outside! Play more! When was the last time you got on a swing? Go hop on one soon, you'll thank yourself for it. When I became more active, lost weight, and got out of my head, my self-doubt went away. My life improved dramatically. I am one of the happiest people I know :o) If music brings you joy, play more of it. If Ice cream is your favorite thing in the world to put into your mouth, DO IT, just know that every action we take (or don't take) can bring us closer to, or push us away from that happiness we are all always looking to find more of.

When your team can play with each other, status levels drop, communication widens, and true bonds are formed. Breakroom Basketball, Ice cream snack day, and even just talking around the water cooler is playtime at work. Outings are healthy. Mandatory team interactive events, and fun staff development team bonding sessions where cooperation is highlighted or teamwork is needed to succeed and complete the game or mission at hand.

Brainstorming - Stream of Consciousness - Trust

Creative development has been one of the most satisfying works of my career. When someone has an idea, but they just don't know how to execute or develop it into something tangible. Something that can be an asset for sale, building something from a few words on paper into a full-scale endeavor feels good. Creativity needs to flow.

Before I ever became an improviser, I watched my father go through a process of flushing out ideas. He would then wash his hands and leave the bathroom ready to go. Once I became an improviser, I was able to utilize the skill set he taught me as a producer/salesman, but also that confidence in trusting whatever my mind comes up with. I've learned not to put a governor on the spicket.

I let whatever comes out, come out. In doing this, my teammates and I have been able to explore and uncover ideas, angles, and options that may not have been thought of.

I have found free-flowing word association a great way to find jump-off points for new ideas, innovation, creativity, and for me most of all humor. When you include everyone on your team in a brainstorming session, it allows everyone to feel as though they have skin in the game, especially if one of their ideas is valid and worthy of exploring.

As a Neurodiverse person, I find it enlightening to see that the corporate world has begun to embrace Neurodivergent employees. They have unique brains and abilities that we cannot see. Some of these abilities are far superior to the average brain.

When everyone feels included, it's good. When everyone feels that they can contribute, it's good. When everyone feels heard and acknowledged it's good. Wouldn't it be silly not to tap into all of these different brains with different viewpoints and different conscious existence?

Think about your business being a network processing system, each person on the team has their own BOSS. Would it also make sense that if you were to connect all of these individual processing systems, wouldn't you see more creative ideas, unearth alternative options and a much wider field of view will develop and encourage creativity? Brainstorming alone can be very positive and productive. Brainstorming with others can turbocharge that production.

When you are linking networks together, you must be aware of the possibility of a virus appearing. In this story that virus could be one of the members of the team. This process is an excellent way to weed out those that are not in line with the values and purpose of whatever IT is that you're working on.

Championships are won with a cohesive team working well together. You can buy players, but it doesn't matter how excellent they are as individuals if they don't work well with every individual you have on the court or the field. While I'm using Sports as a comparison, the perfect example is the highest-paid team fielded in the history of Major League Baseball. 2023 New York Mets. They sucked. Can you tell I'm bitter. LGM!

Trust in your team. Work consciously in the present as a unified team, you will surpass whatever you feel is accomplishable. Trust in yourself. Trust in your ideas. Trust in your team to help you succeed.

Business Tips

Connection

First impressions are important. Look nice, smell good, and if you do need to burp, don't blow it out of your mouth and say "Hey, check it out, hot dog breath". When I first entered the entertainment biz, I was told "Always be there 15 minutes early. If you just get there on time, you're late". People hate waiting for others. It sucks. If you are late a lot, maybe set an alarm to help ensure you arrive early. Others depend on you. I do my best to never be late. If you find yourself constantly late for stuff, don't bullshit yourself, know it is a choice. Unless you don't care. If so, then that may be the problem.

How does it feel when you are waiting for someone late? Nuff said. If you are up for it, decide right now and say this out loud.

"Unless it is beyond my control, I will NOT be late anymore.
It's inconsiderate and it isn't new news to me"

Great. Now stick to your word. Now, GO! Go close a deal.

Memorizing Presentations

I could give you a few tips for memorizing, but to me, the best way is to visualize it. You already know this stuff. You are the one chosen to present it. When you present, be present! Do not get caught in your head thinking about the words. Feel the passion of expressing your thoughts and trusting in your ability and knowledge. When I had pages to memorize, I would record myself and play it back on a loop. While reading each word, I visualize each word scrolling in Times Square, one letter at a time. Immerse yourself in what you want to say. You already know it. You know why you are saying it and to quote the Beastie Boys "Let it flow. Let yourself go". Yo...Word!

One Winning Evergreen Sales Tip

Not knowing if alcohol plays a negative part in someone's life, instead of sending a bottle of wine or champagne, I chose to send cold milk and warm cookies. That can solidify a deal and a long-lasting Relationship.

Forget the Expressway...Take the Scenic Route

When I first started producing...I mean selling, my goal was to get that deal. To bring in some money even if I was just getting 15 to 20% of every dollar I brought in. I would try to get straight to the top guy or gal and pitch them. From the moment I got them on the phone I was like a bulldog. I didn't give them much space to speak until I was done with my pitch. Sometimes I'd still get the sale, but the connection was purely based on business. I had a fairly good product to sell, and it was extremely limited to one person or company per category.

Years passed hours of sitting silently on mute, listening to my father schmooze his way into making things happen. Things he didn't even know he was going to make happen, but somehow, he would get the deal. The first thing I noticed that was obvious to me was that he didn't spend that much time talking about the deal, the business, or the money. It would go left; it would go right by the time he got off the phone he would know the history of the other person. Do they have kids? What major league team do they root for, or are they side sleepers? Do they like chocolate or vanilla? Let's Go Mets!

I eventually coined the phrase take the scenic route, not the expressway. When you go straight for the kill to make that sale, you're missing an opportunity to truly bond and connect with this potential prospect/new client, or even better, your new friend. Take the time to get to know them first and you will see the benefits of real connection each time you speak to each other.

Curtain Call:
Wrapping Up with I.T. Exercises

Chapter 7
Practice Exercises & Games

* * *

Working Out Your Brain

Weightlifting and physical exercise can build the muscles in your body; One way to exercise your brain is to play games. Improvisational Thinking, exercises, and games do the same for your mind. Either in a group setting, on a one-on-one basis, or even when rocking them solo, you can work/play with others and grow your mind muscles. This is a workout that you will enjoy, a brain workout.

Improvisational-based exercises force the mind to work fast. It is Impressive when quick-witted lines are spoken. This quick wit ability helps us to connect with others. Tapping into the skills gained through Improvisational training helps you think faster and act on your feet swiftly. In trusting your gut's initial instincts, you can allow your imagination and instant thought impulses to see the light of day. You will open up your mind, gain confidence, and awaken your inner child.

There are no rules. There are no props or machines needed. There is no such thing as right or wrong in this healthy, creativity-enhancing, and innovative improvising methodology. The main component is being completely present and in the moment. This way, any self-limiting thoughts and wasteful self-judgment rising, cannot get in the way of a good workout and having fun.

After years of study, in article from the Harvard Business Review written by Roderick Gilkey and Clint Kilts scientifically proved that play keeps you healthy and happy.

Here are some of their smarter, fancy, more clinical words explaining it:

"Play engages and works the prefrontal cortex, responsible for your highest-level of cognitive functioning – including self-knowledge, accessing your memory, mental imagery, and incentive and reward processing…Besides the Improvisational games and exercises, activities like bridge, chess, sudoku, role-playing games, and challenging crossword puzzles all provide rigorous neural workouts".

Experience more of your own life as it happens. Everyone loves to play games. These games have no pieces to lose, no spinners, or dice. Quick Wit Improvisational games are a great way to spend family time. Being present. Stop Thinking and Start Being!

Why don't more people try improv? Because they are shy…they believe you have to think fast…they don't think they are funny. Improv is acting in the moment without knowing the plan. It's that simple. Each of us is improving every day by experiencing and responding in the moment. Being in the moment is different than living in the moment. I am not talking about jumping out of a plane, bungee jumping, or partying till you pass out. No. I am talking about being present.

Getting caught up in fantasy thinking, thoughts can consume your will. Fill your head with resentments, regrets, and maybe even remorse. Or they get caught up in the Fear, Anxiety, and anticipation of unknown tomorrows.

I hope you begin to introduce the magic of Improvisational Thinking, quick wit, and improv games into your daily life. We have trained and worked with people of all ages and from all walks of life. Kids to Senior Citizens and everyone in between, from CEOs to Janitors. It's all the same.

Through innovative, thought-provoking, mind training, you can learn to use the skills and core principles of Improv. Your comfort level will be raised, your ability to respond will increase, and you will take more risks and challenge the status quo. You will find yourself smiling more often and a great byproduct of this training…your humorous side will be revealed more often than your grumpy side. If you want to enjoy your family time and be happier more consistently, incorporate these exercises, stay present, and win the day.

Remember, Happiness is not a location you can drive to. It is a state of mind. We simply want more of those moments of happiness. Open your mind and trust in yourself. Go Play!

Icebreakers and Warm-ups

Every workshop I facilitate begins with an icebreaker. It's a warm-up exercise that always leads to a room full of smiles. Remember to always start strong. Initially, the goal is to have the participants accept this new experience and begin to let go of ego and status. These warm-up exercises get the participants up on their feet. Their blood gets pumping and they begin to challenge their comfort zone. We will then wake up creativity, intuitiveness, and spontaneity and learn how to "NOT OVER THINK … AND PREPARE TO REACT". This helps us to get out of our heads, conquer fear/shyness, and help to become more aware and present, to sharpen our ability to respond to the unexpected with more creativity and confident communication.

Below is a list with the names, some of the value/benefits, and introduction to the rules of the icebreaker, game, or exercise. Feel free to dive right in. You can also search YouTube to find examples of these games. Remember skill levels vary so some videos may not hit it out of the park, but they should serve as an example and give you a taste. You will quickly see the value of exercising your mind. By increasing your mental agility through improvisational workouts and incorporating humor into your daily lives, you will become more comfortable dealing with the unknown.

I have been told: "Ever since I started playing these warm-up games and exercises, I feel like the wind is now at my back", "This stuff now helps me breeze through those uncomfortable experiences I would typically shy away from due to fear and anxiety". "Can you please put on pants?" (ok maybe not this last one).

I mentioned this in an earlier chapter, but it is worth repeating. In most cases, I like to challenge myself and say yes to almost everything. I then gather as much information as I can, and then, if necessary, I can politely say No.

Crazy 8's

This is a great game to get everyone up and energized. The leader is going to start by raising their right hand. Everyone follows. At this point the leader and everyone else counts in rhythm out loud to eight; shaking their right hand eight times. Then, without any beat missed, immediately the left arm goes up and you shake the left hand eight times. Onto the right leg shake your foot eight times. Same with the left leg and foot. Now repeat the process with the number seven. As you continue to six times, then five times, you should slowly speed it up with each number. By the time you're at one, everyone looks like screaming, arm and leg waving, raving lunatics. If you look around the room, I will promise you there will not be one person that is not smiling.

Head, Shoulders, Knees and Toes

The name of the game says it all. It's the old Children's Classic. Play by doing each movement as it is said in the song. Get quicker as you go.

Head, shoulders, knees and toes, knees and toes. Head shoulders, knees and toes, knees, and toes. Eyes and ears and mouth and nose. Head, shoulders, knees and toes, knees, and toes.

My Bonnie

My Bonnie is a game that is played by everyone singing the classic song, "My Bonnie". If people don't know it, quickly teach them, by singing a verse. As the song is being sung, each time a word that starts with a B is said, you stand up (or sit down). The next B word you sit down, the next B word you stand up, etc.

My **B**onnie lies over the ocean.

My **B**onnie lies over the sea.

My **B**onnie lies over the ocean,

So, **B**ring **B**ack my **B**onnie to me.

Bring **B**ack, **B**ring **B**ack

O **B**ring **B**ack my **B**onnie to me to me

Bring **B**ack O **B**ring **B**ack.

O **B**ring **B**ack my **B**onnie to me.

This is an extremely successful icebreaker. It is helpful if whoever is leading it, masters the up/down pattern. Once you're complete and you look around, I will guarantee there will not be one face without a smile. Why? Because every single one of them just looked extremely silly…together! The leader gets the best view as they get to witness the mayhem of how far from in sync the group is. When I see the sea of extremely out of sync humans missing the mark over and over again, I find it hilarious every time.

Zip Zap Zup

Warm Up, Focused Communication, Eye Contact, Concentration

Start the game by pointing at another player in the circle and saying "Zip." That player, with no hesitation, must immediately point to another player and say "Zap." That player must, in turn, immediately point to another person and say "Zup." And that person must immediately point to someone else and say "Zip." Continue in this fashion until someone makes a mistake by either saying the wrong word or by hesitating too long. When that happens, all grab hands (or No touch - just throw hands up), Raise them close in on the circle, and say Ahh Ooo Gah! Start Again Zip Zap Zup Zip Zap Zup Zip Zap Zup Zip Zap Zup Zip Zap Zup Zap…Aaa Ooo Gah! Restart: Zip Zap Zup Zip Zap Zup Zip Zap Zup Zip Zap Zup Zip Zap Zip…Aaa Ooo Gah

Group Games:

A-Z

Concentration, Listening Skills, Vocabulary, Focused Communication, Justification

This game can be played internally by yourself. It's the best one on one. But, everyone in a circle can work too. It is a difficult exercise, but it's just a basic conversation in the round. The first person begins with the first letter of the alphabet.

Example:

Player 1) **A**bsolutely not! I will not let you have a dog.

Player 2) **B**ut Daddy, I want a Dog.

Player 3) **C**an we have a dog Mommy?

Player 4) **D**idn't your father already say no?

Player 5) **E**very time I ask you for something you say no!

Player 6) **F**rannie, I will not talk about it again.

Player 7) **G**o do your homework and leave me alone...etc.

After they establish the game, a conductor can be selected to step into the circle and point to the next person randomly...so again they must be paying attention and listening as it must make sense, and they have no clue if they are next. If you get stuck, say any word that starts with your letter. Or just make up any word and find your way back to the topic.

Player 8) **H**orbischloop...is the name of the puppy my friend Wooggie will give me! For free!!

Bus Stop

This game is a play on the "Make me Laugh" concept. One person sits in a chair. Everyone else lines up. One at a time, they have 5 seconds to 1 minute to get the person in the chair to laugh. If the entire group finishes without getting a laugh, the second round is to get a smile. If I can register a dimple, I'll call the smile. When someone gets the laugh, they sit in the chair and the next person starts the line again.

Conducted Story

Focused Concentration & Attention, Synergy, Listening, Creative Thinking

Everyone participates. Together, create a story. A story that has never been told before and will never be told again. It is set up as a "One time only event". The story must make sense. It is all about focusing attention on the moment and listening clearly to what is being said. It creates one group mind. First, we all clear our minds as no one can play this game if they are thinking about what they want to say. We can all see who is thinking too much as they attempt to force their idea into the story. They must focus their attention on The Conductor. They must be looking directly at the Conductor and listening to what the other player(s) is saying so they will know where to pick up. The Conductor directs the game by pointing to a player. As long as The Conductor is pointing to that player, that player continues to speak. The moment The Conductor moves their hand away, that player must immediately stop speaking...even if it is in the middle of a word. The Conductor will then randomly move onto another player. Therefore, they have no idea when they will be called. This reinforces the need to be paying close attention to what is being said. If The Conductor cuts someone off mid-word, the next player must finish the word.

Example: Player 1) Noah was on his way to schoo...Player 2)...ool on the big yellow bus. The timing of the conductor is very important. Cutting people off mid-word can lead to some fun and surprising laughs.

For example, Julie says we were going to st...The conductor points to someone else now they have many choices to finish that

144

word and send the story in a completely different direction. Julie was going to say we were going to St...ephanie's house to cook a feast, but instead, the conductor pointed to James, who said st...ay up all night watching YouTubes. Or to Mike, st...omp on that cockroach. It's fun to conduct because you get the opportunity to send it to someone else to see what happens next. For example, Susan says, once upon a time there was a... She was about to say princess, but instead, the conductor quickly points to Dave who says ... Hockeyplayer named...Todd. Todd has blue...Blood...He is rich ...etc.

Everyone must be aware as the next player could switch it up. The game continues for a while...until The Conductor senses its time and changes the rules to another version. That's next.

Conducted Story: One - Word

Similar to Story, but in version two. The conductor only allows them to say one (1) word at a time. *Faster pace and better listening.* This is One-Word-Story. The name says it all. It can be done in a circle, One on One, or like the story, it can be conducted randomly making it much harder to get lost in your head.

1. Once
2. Upon
3. A
4. Time
5. There
6. Was
7. Twelve
8. Goldfish
9. Flying

You can also do it as a 2 or 3-word story.

Entrances & Exits:

THIS ROLE-PLAYING IMPROV GAME FORCES CREATIVITY.
BY MAKING PRETEND SCENES / SKETCHES / SCENARIO

*Letting Go and Acceptance of New Ideas, Creative
Thinking, and Emotional Response*

One or Two participants start up front and begin a scene. This scene is not planned and no setup is given. It simply begins with a statement as a launching point. After a few moments, and the scene is underway, a third player enters the scene with something completely different. Immediately the two players drop who and whatever they were doing and accept what the third player has brought in. It shouldn't relate to the first scene at all.

Then, after a few beats, the player who has been on the stage the longest must justify a reason to exit the scene. Once that player exits and only two remain, the next person online enters with yet another COMPLETELY DIFFERENT scenario. Repeat previous directions. Example:

Player 1) says "I have tickets to the Taylor Swift concert!"

Player 2) takes it and adds "Awesome, I tried but couldn't get any!"

Player 1) I know that's why I got TWO!

Player 2) OMG! You are the best friend ever!

Player 1) I know

...at any point the next player in line enters with:

Player 3) "I am sorry to say, but I ate half of your dog" Now #1 & 2 must completely drop the topic of Taylor Swift and deal with the new topic of their friend eating poor Fluffy.

The other two might say

2) "But Fluffy was my best friend"

1) "I always hated that dog!".

Now the player who has been in the longest must justify a reason to leave…they cannot just run off…#1 Must justify an exit here. He/she might say, "I am hungry too…I'm gonna go finish the other half". (exit).

The two remaining players continue for a moment until the next online enters with something COMPLETELY DIFFERENT.

4) "I did it, I signed up. I'm joining the Navy!"

We do not enter with a question and in fact, do our best to avoid asking questions throughout. We build on the tenet of YES, AND! This is the core of scene building.

Experts

Confidence Building, Confront Shyness, Creative Reactive Response Skills, Spontaneity

All of the participants are experts…the only problem is, that they have no clue as to what their specific expertise is. It is set up similar to a press conference. The other participants raise their arms and once selected they bombard the expert with ridiculous questions. The key is to answer the question immediately with no hesitation. The truth is, the answer can be just as ridiculous as the question, but it must make sense and it must be answered with creativity and complete confidence.

Freeze Tag:

Creative Thinking, Physical Justification, Humor, Finding Truth In Physical Communication

Two players start an improvised scene. The others line up. At any point in time, the next player in line can call Freeze. The first two must instantly freeze in whatever position they are in. The new player then either joins in or tags out one of the 2 players and takes his or her place. Both players then start a new scene, justifying their positions. BLIND VARIATION: We then raise the stakes; I have the line turn around and face their backs to the action. This way the next player does not know what position they will have to take when they get pushed in the game, and hence are less prepared, and crazier, more exciting stuff tends to happen.

Hot Spot

This musical game was played in the film Pitch Perfect. Everyone circles up. One player steps into the circle and starts singing a known song. Make it clear it does not have to be sung well, just do their best and have fun. As soon as this player shows any signs of stopping (because she doesn't know the lines anymore, gets tired or embarrassed) another player needs to step in and take over by singing a different song that was inspired by a word, or a lyric from the previous song.

Example:

You are my sunshine, my only sunshine. You make me happy when skies are grey…

You are the sunshine of my life. That's why I'll always be around

I'm walking on Sunshine, Whoa Oh… I'm walking on Sunshine, Whoa Oh

Walking in a winter wonderland

Your Body is a wonderland

Move your body Yeah Yeah, etc.…

This exercise is not about improvising songs, but more of a group thing. Players need to know that the group will support them when they're out of breath. The idea is to keep singing.

Object Freeze (aka Props):

Acting on Instinct, Creative Thinking, Focused Concentration, Humor

A similar game is played on the show "Whose Line is it Anyway?" It's called Props. A player is handed an object. They do a short character scene or even just one line using the object as something it is not, but its shape, texture, color, and insinuated usage suggest or inspire something to use it for. Another player jumps in to replace that player. Everyone continues to take turns using the object as something else entirely. And so on…

Sometimes if they are tough enough, use a whistle if it is worthy, or if it is weak quack. A real whistle and duck call are helpful but not essential.

Examples:

- A Lighter - Using it to light an invisible cigar is NO GOOD. It is a lighter. QUACK
- Pretending to bounce it like a basketball QUACK, nothing about a lighter can be seen as round, orange, bounceable.

- But if you hold and light it over your head and cleverly say -

"Look, a prehistoric idea." WHISTLE! You may even get a laugh.

- A toothpick - Say it's a pool cue stick for a hamster WHISTLE!
- A pair of gloves - Hold one under your chin and the other one on top of your head and say: Cock-a-doodle-do. WHISTLE!
- A bottle of water - Place it on the ground. Start beating your chest as you speak like a helicopter pilot saying: If you look down there to the left, you can see the Empire State Building. WHISTLE!

Questions

Questions is an extremely difficult game. It truly puts your mind on the spot. The game is quite simple, but not easy. You are only allowed to ask questions. No statements are allowed. The difficulty is in the fact that each sentence is a question and we naturally want to answer that question. You are not allowed to answer a question with the statement in this game, only another question.

Example:

1. How did you like that party last night?
2. What party?
3. Wait, you didn't get an invitation?
4. You weren't invited?
5. You don't know what happened between me and Steve?
6. What happened between you and Steve?
7. Do you remember the concert Steve took me to?

8. Are you gonna tell me you still haven't paid him back yet?
9. How do you know I owe him money?
10. Don't you owe everyone money?

If the answer to that question is

11. Yeah, I guess I do."

We would stop the game. That is a statement... it's funny, but... YOU'RE OUT!

You can just start again. This game can be played as a one-on-one. You can line up, and as somebody messes up, the next person takes their place. This is also a simple mind-building exercise you can do in your head while walking or relaxing. It is truly a great brain workout.

Rhyming Verse:

Rhyming & Rhythmic Skills, Musical Sensibility, Concentration, Listening, and Creative Thinking

This game may sound like a Dr. Seuss story. You can play with no tempo at all by just working the rhymes. You can add a slow rhythmic toe tap or a beat. Amp it up by playing a karaoke track to any musical style. You can usually lower the playback speed to go with a beginner level.

1st player starts with a single line:

My name is Adam and I like to bake'

2nd Player finishes that line and starts one:

If you would like, I will make you a cake

2nd Player Continues by starting a new one:

What kind would you like, will chocolate do?

3rd Player finishes and starts one:

Yes, in fact, will you make me two?

3rd Did you run out of chocolate?

That is not good

4th Player finishes and starts one:

If you can do Vanilla, I think you should

4th You don't like vanilla? It's banana you'd like?

5th Player finishes and starts one:

I'll have to go get some from my neighbor Spike…

Yada Yada Yada. etc.

What Are You Doing:

Right / Left Brain workout, Concentration, Listening Skills, and Creative Thinking

This exercise is extremely difficult. We work with both the left and right sides of the brain.

Player 1) Begins by making a physical motion.

Example: Brushing my hair.

Player 2) says "What are you doing". Player 1) must say something other than what they are doing physically. Something like: "Tying my shoe". Player 2) starts to tie their shoe. Player 1) says what are you doing? Player 2) must again say something other than what they are doing. "Kicking a tire" ...etc. There are three fouls.

Similar Action (aka Looks Like) – If they are physically brushing their hair, they cannot say: "Checking my head for lice " because the action you are already doing looks like you may be checking for lice.

Repetition – If one player had said Brushing my hair already, a player cannot say: Brushing my teeth or brushing my cat...Brushing Brushing Brushing is a repeat from earlier.

Hesitation – If a player does not come out with the action quick enough and uses a mechanism to stall (Example: I aaaaaaaam...or...Oh, well...I...am...). When a player makes an error, the entire group says: "You are (claps their hands twice CLAP CLAP) ...out of here"! The next player in line steps in and the game resumes.

Yes, And...

Saying No will usually put a halt to whatever it is you are saying not to do. In this game, as if it was an Ad Agency Pitch, based on an audience suggestion, 2 people come up and sell us on a great new idea (they did not know about it until now!) One makes a statement...the other says yes, and ...adds more...then the other does the same by saying yes and ...and adding more.

This is a great exercise to help you get into the habit of saying yes!

153

Examples:

This will be the best campaign ever!

Yes! And…It will have a big celebrity in it!

Yes! And…They will be wearing a chicken suit!

Yes! And…They'll be riding a unicycle.

Yes! And…We will have them juggling torches of fire!

Yes! And…

Etc.

1 – 10:

Concentration, Group Mind, Selfishness, Sharing, Give and Take, Risk Taking, and Teamwork.

THIS GAME IS A GREAT CLOSER. IT WORKS WHEN YOU ALL WORK TOGETHER.

All players lower their heads and close their eyes. One player starts by saying 1. Another says 2…and so on. The problem is, nobody knows who is going to speak next. If more than one voice is heard saying a number, we start again at 1…until we can get to 10 or more.

The Joy of Energetic Practice

Learning doesn't have to be a dry, monotonous affair. "Beuller? Beuller? Anyone? Anyone? It can be joyfully fun & funny, mind-blowing, and even exhilarating. That's where enjoyably energetic practices come into play. They're not just about injecting fun into your training; they create a relaxed and supportive learning environment.

These practices are designed to encourage creativity, teamwork, true relationship building/bonding, stronger connections, and a willingness to risk thinking outside the box—qualities that can set you apart in your personal life, business and increase your ability to sell IT.

So, get ready to embrace the joy of learning how to be more comfortable when you must fly by the seat of your pants on the spot. You can accomplish it much better through the understanding of Improvisational Thinking.

Chapter 8
Perfect Just the Way We Are

* * *

My World - My Story, is Your Story

The main cast in my world begins and ends with the love of my life, my wife Melissa. I met her on a late Saturday night. It was her birthday, 12:01 am. She didn't know who I was. I had just been given her phone number by our big sisters. After singing her a special birthday song and immediately hanging up, I called her back and we spoke until 3 am. We had our first date that Monday. Our second date came…nine months later. A long story, for another time. I can say this…after date two, we have not been apart. Melissa (aka MYlissa) is the mother of the three best creations I've ever been a part of. Sophie, Noah and BenJamin. She is not only the best mother to my kids, but she is also a fantastic partner, friend, Top Chef, House CEO, and the Glue. She is my rock. She is my strength; she is my smile! Thank you, I love you!

Besides my phenomenal wife, improving my life, I must mention her assistance in creating our three delicious children.

Sophie is a chip off the old block. Right from wrong is very important to her and just know, she is right. She'll be graduating from university as a presidential list scholar. (Holy cannoli! That is not inherited from my genes.) She has the voice of an angel and I am sure she could run for president and win easily.

My middleman is Noah. He is a dashing 6-footer. He is a natural entrepreneur. His first business was selling bubble gum for 4 x his cost. He has had Lunar Occulitis for years. His good friends created the https://www.lunaroec.org website…Lunar Occulitis Education Center. He cannot see the moon? He is also musically, gifted and a true gentleman.

My baby boy is BenJamin. That's right we pronounce it, Ben Jamin! He's the baby brother that I'm fairly confident will eventually be the big brother to both of his older siblings. This one had big paws at birth. I have a feeling he's gonna be taller than Noah. Noah doesn't agree with that prediction. Ben is the drummer & MMA athlete of the family and perhaps the politician. He was just voted in as treasurer of his High School Class of 2027.

All three of my children are perfect and they've never done anything wrong. I hope you're laughing too.

My parents. Marilyn and Seymour Sietz. Truly the greatest parents a kid could ever ask for. Kind, nurturing, wise, compassionate, inclusive, funny, generous, strong, open, etc.

My mother was the main source of building my confidence in myself; always in my corner supporting and guiding me through the difficult times in life. She fought for me when some educators didn't.

Mom embraced my ADHD and pushed me when I didn't want to jump in. She was also funny and smart and the perfect "Jewish" mother. Just the right mix of "Adam, you can do anything!", "Adam, you are so handsome." and "Adam! Get off of your ass and take out the garbage now before I rip off your arm and beat you with the bloody stump!" She is gone now, but I still smile when I think of her. And yes, that is an actual quote.

My Father was the greatest, kindest, most talented person I've ever met. He was a creative communicator, mentor of the funny, and master of relating to all people. You always felt worthy and important. I hate that his grandchildren never got the opportunity to meet him, but I can feel his spirit surrounding us. I/We miss him at this very moment and every day!

My two sisters Patti and Pamela. The best little sisters a brother could ask for, even if I am the youngest. They were my first audience. First to laugh, first to boo, and first to hang my stuffed animal, cover it in ketchup and say "Look boo boo's dead!" Through thicker or thinner, both have always been there to root me on.

Patti is a brilliant Emmy Award-winning editor (Nominated for two more as I write this). She lives close by, so I get to see her often. She is also the best car sitter of all time. She is the first to tell you she is a connoisseur of Cannabis. She has an alarm set that goes off at 420 every day.

Pamela aka Aunt Lala was like my second mother. When my mom went back to work, Pam was responsible for making sure I got home, did my homework, and didn't breathe, speak, or g-d forbid get in her way. She was my best friend, then my sassy sister who at times, became a little brother terrorist.

Everything changed when I hit 14. Literally. I hit her back for the first time. On that day, a new sheriff arrived in town, Me. We are all very close and our kids love each other the same way.

Jamie is my brother (by Choice). We came into each other's lives at a pivotal time. We were both figuring out what we wanted to do when we grew up. We are still figuring that out.

He has been my listening ear and shoulder to lean on whenever needed. We adopted each other in our late teens. He housed me when I worked for the Mets and Channel 9. We lost our dads one year apart. He ended up going to the same school, The New

Schools Global Village for Video Production. Today, he is an award-winning photojournalist with CNN.

He is a married daddy now, so we get to play together with our wives and children. We have also both doomed our children to be Mets & Jets fans. Ouch! Is that abuse?

My Mother and father-in-law, Joe and Estelle Trachtenberg. With my mother living in South Florida and my father now gone more than two decades, these two fantastic people have been my northern champions.

Grampy Joe, a WWII veteran and former trial attorney has always given some of the best advice (for life and any question on the legalities of business). His stories could be made into movies. I see a younger James Caan playing him. Maybe the Rock.

Grammy Estelle is the last of 6 children. 4 older brothers and one little sister. Today, all are gone along with Grampy Joe, but at 95 she is still herself. She lives with us and brightens our mornings every day. She has always been a strong guide of reason and a master of letting the less-than-wonderful "Stuff" roll off her shoulders. She can accept the unacceptable better than anyone else I've ever known. Together, they've always been supportive, loving, helpful, and storytellers to my children. It has been a great pleasure to truly get to know the two people who gave me the greatest gift I've ever received…My wife, Mylissa. They also birthed what turned out to be a Special Bonus, Holl's and Nance!

I met Buddy Bolton in Florida. He is the most giving, selfless person on earth. Buddy was already a well-known actor in the South Florida market when he auditioned for our troupe, but he was also playing with another group, so we couldn't keep him. Buddy has been my partner on the funny for now over two decades. He was on Conan, and won the Def Comedy Jam. He played the creepy character, The Dentist on Gotham.

The son of pioneering feminist Roxcy Bolton, he tells a story of being a child marching with his mother cheering "My Vagina! My Choice!" So, how could he not be funny? When he moved to NYC six months before I did, he blazed a trail.

When I moved up, he asked me to join his sketch troupe and helped get me stage time. Buddy somehow got the Comic Strip's (gatekeeper) Lucien Hold to pass me without having to go through their stringent lottery or auditioning system. Once Lucien allowed me on that stage, I was in! I was a true Stand-Up Comic. Together we founded Big Hug Productions, ate a lot of cheesy grits, and made a whole lot of the funny.

Pat "The Vampire" Batistini is my mentor and improv guru. After my father passed, I decided I wanted to start a sketch comedy troupe. Something in the style of Monty Python meets Benny Hill topped with some SNL, SCTV, and a drizzle of Kids in the Hall. Pat gave me my nickname, Adam "One" Sietz "Fitz All" and started me on the path to finding my life's purpose. My reason for being. My why!

When I started on the stage I received big laughs, but I was a complete amateur. I was filled with an inflated ego and a need to look cool at all times. Pat was a great teacher and truly helped to break those bad habits.

Then came Bobby "Big" MacDougald and Danny "Speedy" Gonzalez. Both are gone and the world is dimmer without them in it. The four of us truly meshed into a perfect quartet of funny.

I had the great pleasure of working, playing, performing, teaching, coaching, and avoiding many wonderful people.

I love to share the Jedi ways of Improvisational Thinking. Guiding a group of CEOs, or seasoned Grandparents. Sellers of "various kinds of stuff". My favorite? An audience of joyful children. I could go on and on. So many lives have touched my soul and helped guide me through it all. So many others who know they are important to me, but my aging feeble mind cannot remember who right now.

Finding my Voice

I always wanted to be a cartoon. At a very early age, I was always adept at mimicry and cartoon impressions. Unfortunately, I eventually found out I couldn't be animated. My schoolmates first drilled me on my Muppet voices. "Do Kermit Adam...Do Kermit!" Then came the song parodies and eventually characters of my own. From Fat Tony to Fabrice, I would bank experiences and voices. I was developing an act and I didn't even know it.

At nine years old, I wrote, co-directed, and starred in my own original third grade school play: "Yes there is a Santa Clause". I made sure to include everyone in my class by casting them all...and of course, I cast myself in the role of Santa Claus.

By the time I was in high school (Orwellian Class of 1984), I was also doing singing impressions. Depending on the audience, it could be Louis Armstrong, Mel Torme' or Tom Jones...Or it could be Robert Plant, James Taylor, or Philip Bailey (Earth Wind & Fire). I then picked up on comedy routines and classic comedy sketches. I recall the ease of using voices and bits to quickly have everyone in stitches. I would simply recite Richard Pryor, Steve Martin, Sam Kinesin, or Steven Wright's stand-up act. I was hooked on the National Lampoon radio hour and Saturday Night Live. It was through my love of Monty Python, that I taught myself to do an Englishman and cockney woman. Cheech & Chong gave me my Mexican American. I knew almost all of these sketches word for word. Andrew "Dice" Clay, Richard Lewis, Robert Klein, Eddie Murphy, Robert Shimmel and so many more were my idols.

Richard Pryor even taught me the sound a monkey makes when humping a producer's ear. I always knew this funny stuff was a skill that could serve me well.

When I got divorced from my first wife, I thought to myself: "I better try this now…if I don't, I am going to hate myself by the time I hit 40". On the day of my 40th birthday, I felt not only great satisfaction and validation, but celebrated the realization of a dream. I was standing on a Broadway stage about to make my opening night Broadway debut. Huh? What? How? I have since been blessed to repeat that "opening night on Broadway" experience twice more.

Based on some of the stories you hear about diversity, I've had a cakewalk through life. I was raised in an affluent community. Most of the kids I grew up with also had a privileged upbringing. So, I do understand what I dealt with was only adversity from my perspective and my perception. As I can only speak for myself, my adversity was real and at times difficult to overcome. Growing up labeled disabled with a learning disability was just the beginning. Oh, and being called stupid, fat, or four eyes wasn't helping.

My parents spoiled us. My father, Seymour Lloyd Sietz was born in Brooklyn, NY to a doting yet domineering mother and a quiet, kind father. Just like my father, I was fortunate to have a loving, encouraging, supportive family.

My mother was born into a very different family. Her father Morris was a hard-core gambler. She once came home and saw men carrying their couch out. She asked her brother "Did we get a new couch?" he replied, "Nope. Dad bet it, and lost in a poker game". He eventually gambled his business away. He left the family in shame and died before I was born. She tells stories of finding her mother hysterical and suicidal. Her brothers were much older and were away fighting in World War II. Mom had to grow up fast.

162

That was true adversity.

My dad did very well in business, so we had simple problems. Like having to get up to change the channel on one of the seven televisions in the house. We were very fortunate. Have you ever heard the term being "born with a silver spoon in your mouth"? Mine were disposable. My dog had another dog to lick his…We had money. We had a bidet (bid-ay). Who has a bidet? The first time I went to a public park, I got kicked out for washing my ass in the water fountain. Ok not really, really…not really? My mom was always loving, supportive, and encouraging.

Dad was talented in many ways. He and his brother Arnold learned at a very young age the power of a smile and a laugh. Dad and Barry began performing for family and friends and then at school and temples and churches and eventually found some success on the Borscht Belt. He always enjoyed performing and being adored by a crowd of strangers was an obvious bonus.

My father worked in the city. I say city as if anyone reading this knows which city I am referring to. To me, there was always only one. New York City, the Big Apple. As a commuter, he would typically come home late and I would only have a brief amount of time to play with him. On the weekends he played golf and watched any sport on TV.

I missed my Dad a lot growing up, but when we did spend time together, it was usually a lot of fun. I had the great fortune of getting to work with him every day for about 6 years. He was gone in 1993 at only 63 years old. Way too young. I miss him beyond words.

Sports and Entertainment was the family business. The name of the company was Sports/Entertainment Media Corporation. SEM…for Seymour.

Mom ran state beauty pageants for the Miss Universe and Mrs. America organizations. Life was exciting at times. Life was also quite lonely at times.

My sisters were both older than me, so they had little to no interest in playing with me. I was the obnoxious baby brother. I did develop a strong imaginative ability to amuse myself. I would play out stories and be all the characters. This ability flourished later on when I found improvisational comedy. I can say it was Improv and Stand-up Comedy that altered my life direction.

Surprisingly, research shows that we folks with ADHD are typically very creative. We also make great performers. Improvisation especially. Unfortunately, my Dad passed away in 1993. At that point, his company became my company. My big sister Pamela now worked for me, but that did not change the fact that I could never not be her little brother. We battled way too much. I didn't want to do it anymore. I could have easily kept producing meaningless television, tried to sell cars, bartended, or stripped. Instead, I followed my dreams...and lived them!

I was given the name Adam Lee Sietz by my parents. I didn't have a choice at the time. I can consciously recall wanting a different name. At that time, other than myself, I did not know anyone named Adam. So, I wanted to be John. Yup, I wanted to change my name from the name G-d gave to the first of Mankind...ever, to a name used for a toilet or someone employing a hooker. No offense intended John(s).

Today I love my name. It is me. As I sell myself for a living, I guess it's my brand. I'll go by other names once in a while. Like Mr. Sietz, Sir, Dude, Bro, Honey, Love Chunks, Adz, Daddy, Babe, Big Guy, Hey you, and even ...Bob. But my favorite aka, is Dad.

I was cute enough to date beauty queens, and I wrestled...not the beauty queens, the real stuff. And when I say the real stuff, I don't mean: "Oh yeah...mean Gene! I'm gonna rip off his head and bowl with it! Then steal his Woman!!!"

I loved to wrestle. I was able to get over all the pent-up aggression, frustration, and desire to beat up my big sister, and as I got better, I gained and welcomed a new sense of respect, so I wrestled whenever I could. That's right. I wore a singlet...ok...Stop. No Really, Stop it! Will you please stop imagining me in tight-fitting spandex. It makes me very uncomfortable...Oh wait...maybe it's the Spanks I'm currently wearing.

I only lost one wrestling match in my entire career. But hey...She was really strong.

I Want To, But Don't Do

For years I did what was expected of me. I took out the garbage, I earned a living, and I married a supermodel. When I was finished with university (after one month), I went to work in the TV Production Biz. I worked on NY Mets, Rangers, and Knicks broadcasts, Entertainment Tonight, and Madison Square Garden Network. They covered the Yankees back then, but I worked in the Garden on special events like the Wanamaker Millrose Games, Monster Truck car crushing, and Mud Bog racing. That was a lot of fun and they paid me to do it. Eventually, I went to work in my father's production company selling promotional airtime on network and syndicated television.

When my Dad passed away, it wasn't the same. I didn't want to do it anymore, but what else could I do? This was all I've ever done.

I had the gift of learning from a true sales master, so I am sure, I could have easily become a stock broker, realtor or even a kitten juggler. I could have become an underwear model. But no, instead, I decided to throw caution to the wind and said, "If I don't try this now, I will hate myself by the time I hit 40." I took the leap and followed my dreams.

Until that day with Dad, I'd never even entertained the idea of becoming a performer. How often have you wanted to DO something you would enjoy, but you don't do it? You see the person you find attractive, funny, and kind. You've wanted to talk to this person but never had the courage.

Today is the day, you start walking their way. As you get closer, you chicken out and veer off because you don't want to be rejected. You are not alone; you are not helpless and you will never win if you can't ask for what you want. You could also begin a conversation that develops into dinner, leading to a second meet-up, and bada bing bada boom, you've got yourself a real-life love story. You're taking that chance is a win regardless of the result. You also broke down a wall.

Think of a light switch on your chest. Up is on. Above the switch, it says DO. Below the switch it says NOTHING.

When the switch is on, there is action! You are getting what you want, doing what you want, and living the life you want.

When the switch is set in the down position, it is off. When it's off Nothing happens, anyone could yell at the switch or even throw things at it, but unless you turn it on, nothing will happen.

At ComedySportz, we had a sign on top of the doorway out to the stage. As we walked out, we would all tap it. It said: "Don't Think. DO! So, I did!

- I wanted to be a cartoon! I worked on more than a dozen major kid's cartoon series
- I wanted to work with Woody Allen (before the world called him creepy), I did…twice!
- I wanted to be on Broadway, I was… three times.
- I wanted to be a writer, and I am. I have written this book you're holding, Friars Roast material, International animated kids shows, and friends' online dating profiles.
- I wanted to take down Tony Soprano, I got close…and who knows maybe I did?
- I wanted to be married…I am…twice!
- I wanted to be a father…I am…x 3

Now, I wanted to share my experience of how Improvisational Thinking completely changed my life. Drastically!

I was born with the gift of speaking. I talked…a lot, and at times could not shut up. But I rarely ever spoke up when I should have. I was a chicken. Today speaking and writing my words down have helped me get far in life.

I feel my true purpose for being here on this earth…other than eating burgers, harassing my children and my little (older) sisters…is to assist others, and help them break free of their self-imposed barriers, end the excuses, and to just go for it…whatever their "IT" is. Like I said before, my true why, my reason for being, is to put smiles on faces and help others to do the same. I'll repeat…Today I am living my dream. Why shouldn't you?

Chapter 9
Big Hugs Conclusion

* * *

Find the Gold in I.T.!

The choice of how you react and experience these events determines your state of being.

When I first moved up to New York City, one of my main goals was to try to get on a TV show called Whose Line Is It Anyway? At the time it was a successful British television show that showcased phenomenal improvisers. I had heard they may be doing an American version.

About two years into living in Manhattan I got the call. I was excited to get a callback and even more excited when I made it to the final cut. On Monday at noon, I would be in front of the network's bosses testing to be on the television show.

This is it, my dream gig! I was so excited…for a little less than 24 hours because the next day my manager called and told me that she had good news and bad news. Which did I want to hear first? I said "I guess give me good news first". She said we just got a call from Woody Allen's office. They want to book you directly for a scene with Sean Penn. No audition is needed for direct booking. I was very happy to hear this good news, but then quickly remembered she also has bad news for me, so I said hit me with it. She informed me that it would be on Monday.

My mind is in a whirlwind. What do I do? This is my reason for coming to New York. How can I not do the Whose Line testing? I asked my manager what she thought I should do. She said I can't tell you what to do. That's a decision you will have to make. That was not a decision I was ready to make. I said, what would you do? She had a solid point: one of the top directors in the business has just requested me to work on Monday. On a motion picture. This was a job. This was a paying job. Whose Line is an awesome opportunity, but it's still just an opportunity, there is no guarantee.

I decided I wanted to be in the movies more than I wanted to be on Whose Line. I mean how can I turn down spending a day with Spicoli from Fast Times of Ridgemont High? I was disappointed, but I was accepting. Shit happened.

Two hours later the phone rings. It's my manager. She is calling to tell me to take a seat. I sat down and she began to tell me that Woody does not want me to miss out on the opportunity for Whose Line is it Anyway? He will put me up at 8 a.m. first shot of the day and if I'm not done by 11:30 they will call lunch for me and have a car service get me to ABC and then back to the set after I'm done. Holy shit I'm gonna get to do both? She said: Yes!

Monday morning, I got picked up, went out to the studio and spent about an hour and a half with Sean Penn. At least half of that time I was throwing him up against the wall threatening to break his face. Around 11 o'clock I was wrapped, in a car and they took me to ABC. I then had what I have to say was the best audition I've everhad. The other improvisers that were in were praising me and raving about how well I did, in particular my musical improv.

I had one of the most amazing days of my life; after spending the time on set and then feeling like I was walking on air during that audition, still brings goosebumps every time I think about it.

In the end, I did not get whose line is it anyway… and my storyline was edited out of the film for time.

The moral of this story, every day brings you new challenges which will bring you new upsets, new excitements, new wins, and new losses.

The choice of how you react and experience these events determines your state of being. I could've been devastated by the outcomes of both the Whose Line and Woody events. But I wasn't. I could look back on that and get caught up in the disappointment of not getting what I wanted, but the way I look at it is on that day, I won it all. That was an experience and a story I will have forever.

I was, however, validated about two years later. I was at a party and a gentleman that was in a conversation that I was a part of looked at me and said "Hey, I know you." I did not recognize the face. He said, "I'm sure I know you?" I said, what camp did you go to? He said no that's not it, but I know you? Then it hit him. "Whose Line is it Anyway?!" No, I never made it onto that show. I came close, but it didn't happen. He said I know! I know, I was on the production team and we loved you. You were fantastic. The issue was we needed more diversity. There were five people in the cast and four of them were white men. In the end, the amazing Wayne Brady was the man that got that slot and the talented Denny Siegal was the only NY'er cast. I have to say she was well worthy of it and Wayne deserves every drop of success that's come his way since sharing his brilliance on that show.

It's Your World

Well, we're at the end of this book. I am truly happy. We have both reached this point, you reading it and me writing it. If you were to tell me when I was a kid that there would be a day when I could say "I am an author", I would not have believed you.

I'm sure if you choose to utilize some of the things you've had the opportunity to pick up within these pages, You Will Win.

170

I am far from a perfect human being. I have many flaws. I can, however, say I am a happy person. I am a confident person. I am worthy of success. Now you repeat the same words because it's true. You are perfect exactly the way you are…Today. Tomorrow is another day. If you wanna be better, be better. No one else has the power to create change in you other than YOU. You are the master of your universe.

I will repeat it again: YOU Control Your Thoughts, Your Thoughts DO NOT Control You. I always like to repeat that one a few times to remind you. Just know that YOU are good enough as is. Don't let ego or the desire for status get in your way anymore. Communicate with truth and expel any bullshit from your life. You know where the bullshit is and you know when it's coming from you. The fact that I, a Neurodiverse, morbidly obese college dropout, have been able to accomplish some cool things should show you that it can be done! I never thought I could do it, and today I am living my dream.

Please come and join me.

"Don't be a dreamer, live your dream."

As I say these words, the world is currently in a fragile place. The topics of Politics, Religion, Race, Gender, Income/Debt and more get in the way of true happiness. I know many people are struggling and feel there is no way out of whatever situation is holding them down. Lacking love, not enough money, or even a bed. Stay in the moment and improve on the next one.

"Sometimes you have to go to hell before you get to heaven"
- Steve Miller

18 C Words

I am confident in you. You took action. You picked up this book and not only opened it, you read it to this point. Look at you! Yay! I promise IT works. If you've found value here, please practice IT daily. Your BOSS will use LARRY to make sure you are all PACKED up and ready to shine brightly. Choose to stay present and trust in the power of your BOSS's ability to retain andaccess what you have filed and stored. You've just downloaded and filled in some of the words from these pages. I hope they stick.

You are welcome to share any of this stuff with a friend or loved one or even the stranger in the stall next to you. I say that because I am a sharer and can't help it, I must share any new idea, a new toy, and…any newly released, personally manufactured, methane gas. That's something I am generous to always give away without expecting anything in return (other than some Ozium, Glade or Airwick). When you have completed this book, if you promise yourself, you will follow through and implement IT. If you trust and hold yourself to your word, take actionable accountability, if you stay out of your head and remain on the track. You'll be living here in the life you are living now, not in your head lost in days ahead or days past. You'll espouse the 18 C Words:

"You Can and will gain Comfort and Confidence through Combining Creative Comedy, Committed Concentration, and Truly Connected Collaboration. This enhances your Clarity of Cause, helps you to be Calmer, Cooler, and be a more Captivatingly Commanding Communicator able to Capitalize and Cash in!"

(I know there are 19, but I like the number 18 more. Think of it like a baker's dozen, I threw in an extra C'word.)

172

Let Go and Just Be Yourself!

The world would be much better with more laughter. When you have the opportunity to share and spread smiles please take it. Happiness, laughter, and smiling are all ways to recharge the positive energy that seems to be lacking around the world. When you trust in this hard fact…You have gotten to this day, at this point and you're still alive. Decide to turn your switch on, locate the path you want to follow, and hop on it.

I do promise you this, if you become your own champion you will win. Do not let those negative thoughts or negative people define your state of being. Shit happens, get used to it. Embrace new ways to react and deal with whatever comes your way. Whether it's good shit or the kind that hits the fan, trust that you can handle it.

Improvisational Thinking was the key to changing my life for the better. Remaining present and accountable. Taking more risks, saying yes, and asking for what I want has brought me to this day and the pleasure of knowing you made it here to join me.

It's happening Right NOW! Ok…I'm done…and promise I used the Glade Hawaiian tropical fresh powder scent.

Thank you very much for taking the journey and the time to listen. Let go! Just Be!

Unscripted Success
With
Improvisational Thinking

Adam Lee Sietz

"Mostly"
The ^ True Confessions of a Successful
Former *Really Fat Guy with ADHD Who
(*Currently in Fat Guy Remission)
Vanquished Self Doubt and is Living His Dreams

Secrets of How to Sell It …
…Whatever your "IT" is?

Get Them to Buy into "IT" With a Smile!
IT = Your Idea - Your Product - Your Service - Your Opinion

Adam Sietz Bio

An Award-winning writer/producer turned, Award winning comedian, turned Award winning actor, Adam Sietz has spent the last 35 years performing and producing in the Entertainment Biz. He wrote and starred in his first school play at age 9. Since then, he has written extensively for television, corporate events and various private individuals from Comedians to CEO's. He won a special achievement Emmy award at the ripe old age of 21, produced television shows internationally; performed on Broadway 3 x times; Friars Roast and worked with Woody Allen twice.

In addition to moonlighting as one of NYC's top VO artist's, Adam has performed stand-up and improvisational comedy in clubs and venues the world over. As a cast member, Adam can be seen and heard in programs as diverse as Dora the Explorer, Go Diego Go, and Wonder Pets to Star Wars: Visions, Chappelle's Show, The Sopranos and consistent visits to all of the Law & Order's. He's been in some of the top Video Games of all time, many GTA(s), BioShock, Star Wars: The Old Republic and many others. His best work ever…His 3 delicious children "Sophie, Noah & BenJamin", Co-Created with his beautiful wife Melissa.

While he has won many awards and signed many autographs, he has also changed many diapers, a few tires, and washed many a dish. But maybe most of all, he's had the good fortune to follow three wise words of advice: To "LEARN" then "EARN", and now it's time to "RETURN". With this driving desire to give back, Adam began volunteering at local Schools, Nursing Homes, and Rehabilitation Centers. Before long, he was teaching and training adults and kids ranging from 5yrs. to 95yrs.

Adam is taking his personal brand of silly, Speaking, and Improvisational Thinking on the road to motivate leaders, build team confidence, inject humor, deliver value, increase focus, support each other, and most of all...create Smiles.

Made in the USA
Columbia, SC
23 September 2024

d2bffe66-598b-403f-880e-3d6a10743317R01